To Aaron
Franz
Mmmma

The POTTERSAURUS 1,500 Words
Harry Potter Readers Need To Know

By Eric D. Randall

www.pottersaurus.com

Published by Pinewood Press,
a subsidiary of NYPER Publications
18 Upton Road
Albany, NY 12208

www.pottersaurus.com

Library of Congress Control Number: 2006940818

ISBN-10:   1-878673-35-1
ISBN-13:   978-1-878673-35-0

Cover photo by Lea Dales
www.leadales.com
Cover model: Ana Lanier

Dedication

For Julia Grace Randall
and her Grandpa Harvey
with thanks for all their help
with this book

Introduction and User's Guide

What does it mean to "solemnly" swear that one is up to no good? Although the Harry Potter books are considered children's literature, some of the words that author J.K. Rowling uses are unfamiliar to many young readers (as well as some not-so-young readers). These words are defined in *The Pottersaurus: 1,500 Words Harry Potter Readers Need to Know*.

With *The Pottersaurus*, you will know what Rowling meant when she wrote that Aunt Marge became apoplectic, Percy spoke sanctimoniously or Hermione answered a question pensively. You'll find out what Dumbledore was talking about when he said "oddment" in his opening speech of a few words ("Nitwit! Blubber! Oddment! Tweak!").

The Pottersaurus will help even the most devoted readers see things that they missed in the Potter books. With it, you'll be able to appreciate the humor in Hermione's description of Pansy Parkinson as "thicker than a concussed troll." You'll learn what Ron meant when he accused Hermione of "fraternizing with the enemy" at the Yule Ball and what Bellatrix LeStrange meant when she wondered whether Dumbledore trusts Severus Snape "implicitly." You'll learn the meaning of the word "marauder" (as in "the Marauder's Map") as well as the definition of "maladies" (as in "St. Mungo's Hospital for Magical Maladies and Injuries").

American readers will appreciate that *The Pottersaurus* includes the occasional British term that crops up in the U.S. editions of the series, such as Hagrid's complaint that Dementors give him "the collywobbles."

Each *Pottersaurus* entry includes at least one example of how the word is used in books I-VI of the Harry Potter series.

Only "real" words that are considered part of the English language are included. There are no entries for spells, the names of imaginary magical objects (such as the pensieve) or other terms created by J. K. Rowling.

Some words in the definitions are in *italic*. That means the italicized word is an entry in **The Pottersaurus**. For example:

> Overt - Obvious. Harry notices that Snape seems strangely *wary* of displaying overt *animosity* to Mad-Eye Moody. (GF, Ch. 14)

Because "wary" and "animosity" are both in *italic*, you know that those words are also defined in **The Pottersaurus**.

The notation "(GF, Ch. 14)" in the example above indicates that the word appeared in Chapter 14 of *Harry Potter and the Goblet of Fire*. The following abbreviations are used:

SS = *Harry Potter and the Sorcerer's Stone*

CS = *Harry Potter and the Chamber of Secrets*

PA = *Harry Potter and the Prisoner of Azkaban*

GF = *Harry Potter and the Goblet of Fire*

OP = *Harry Potter and the Order of the Phoenix*

HBP = *Harry Potter and the Half-Blood Prince*

J.K. Rowling obviously loves to use the perfect word. Becoming familiar with these terms will help you improve your own writing ... and come in handy when you take the SAT or ACT! When it comes to expressing ideas, telling a story or taking a college admissions test, a good vocabulary is like magic.

- Eric D. Randall
Albany, N.Y.

Note: Warner Bros. is the owner of all copyrights and trademarks in and to all of the Harry Potter books and movies. *The publisher of* **The Pottersaurus: 1,500 Words Harry Potter Readers Need to Know** *is independent of and not affiliated with J.K. Rowling, Scholastic Books, Carlsen Verlag, Bloomsbury Publishing or Warner Bros.*

Abashed - Embarrassed. Draco Malfoy looks abashed when his father notes that Hermione Granger, "a girl of no wizard family," beat him on every exam. (CS, Ch. 4) After Dumbledore calls Tom Riddle a thief, Riddle does not look even *remotely* abashed. (HBP, Ch. 13)

Abated - Stopped. Harry didn't worry about his possible expulsion from Hogwarts when he was busy cleaning up 12 Grimmauld Place, but his anxieties returned whenever the action abated. (OP, Ch. 6)

Abided - Followed a rule or request. To make it clear that his family always abided the law, Barty Crouch says they used magic carpets only before they were banned. (GF, Ch. 7)

Abject - Utter, complete. Dobby crouches behind Lucius Malfoy with a look of abject terror on his face. (CS, Ch. 18)

Abnormality - The state of being different. Uncle Vernon refers to Harry's ability to do magic as "your abnormality." (PA, Ch. 2)

Abomination - A truly disgusting thing. From her portrait, Sirius Black's mother calls him an abomination. (OP, Ch. 4)

Abruptly - Quickly and sharply. After Mrs. Norris is found petrified, Justin Fitch-Fletchley turns abruptly when he sees Harry in a stairwell. (CS, Ch. 9) Harry speaks abruptly to Riddle when asked how he survived an attack by a powerful wizard when he was just a baby. (CS, Ch. 17)

Abstained - Made a decision not to do something. Prof. McGonagall abstained from assigning homework in the week before Gryffindor and Slytherin were to play Quidditch. (OP, Ch. 19)

Abstinence - Policy of refraining from an activity, usually drinking of alcohol. After the Fat Lady *overindulged* in wine over Christmas, she made "abstinence" the password to enter the Gryffindor Common Room. (HBP, Ch. 17)

Absurd - Ridiculous. Slughorn explains that he is able to sneak into Muggle houses by putting a simple freezing charm on Muggles' absurd burglar alarms. (HBP, Ch. 4)

Abysmal - Incredibly bad. Neville gets an abysmal grade in Potions, but makes up for it with a top grade in Herbology. (SS, Ch. 17)

Accessible - Able to be entered, obtained or used. Dumbledore tells about discovering a room full of *chamber pots* that he thinks may be accessible only at 5:30 a.m., or when the moon is quarter-full, or when the seeker "has an exceptionally full bladder." (GF, Ch. 23)

Accomplice - Partner in crime or mischief. Dumbledore starts to ask Draco who was his accomplice in Hogsmeade, but he figures it out before he finishes the sentence. (HBP, Ch. 27)

Account - Story or explanation. Harry finds himself *besieged* with requests to give a firsthand account of how Dumbledore came to leave Hogwarts and leave Dolores Umbridge in charge. (OP, Ch. 28)

Accusations - Claims that someone has done something wrong. Prof. Trelawney says Dolores Umbridge's inspection report is full of unfounded accusations. (OP, Ch. 17)

Accusatory - In a challenging and critical way. Ron questions Cho Chang about her favorite Quidditch team in a *tactless* and accusatory way; he suggests that she began rooting for her favorite team only after it began winning. (OP, Ch. 12)

Accustomed - Used to. Prof. McGonagall says she's become accustomed to having the Quidditch Cup in her study and that she didn't want to have to turn it over to Prof. Snape. (OP, Ch. 19)

Addled - Put into a state of confusion. Malfoy tells Ron that Mr. Weasley appears destined for a St. Mungo's ward that serves people whose brains have been addled by magic; the comment upsets Neville greatly. (OP, Ch. 17) Dumbledore says Harry is sane and that his scar has not addled his brain. (GF, Ch. 36) Rufus Scrimgeour tells the Prime Minister that the reason that a government official has been quacking like a duck is that a curse has addled his brains. (HBP, Ch. 1)

Addressee - Person to whom a letter is addressed. Ron scolds Pidwidgeon for cruising around Hogwarts with a letter strapped to his leg, saying, "You bring letters to the addressee! You don't hang around showing off!" (GF, Ch. 21)

Adept - Skilled. Snape's comment upon beginning teaching Occlumency to Harry is that he hopes Harry is more adept at it than potions. (OP, Ch. 24)

Admonitions - Warnings. Hermione keeps up a stream of admonitions to try to *dissuade* Harry from his plan to break into Umbridge's office, so he can use her fireplace to communicate with Sirius. (OP, Ch. 29)

Admonitory - Cautioning. An owl gives an admonitory hoot as it waits for Cho Chang to attach a parcel. (OP, Ch. 13) An old chimney rises above Severus Snape's house like an admonitory finger. (HBP, Ch.2)

Adorned - Decorated with. At the Quidditch World Cup, you could buy a tie adorned with a picture of a lion that actually roared. (GF, Ch. 7)

Adrenaline - A chemical produced by the body that stimulates alertness and energy in people. After battling a dragon, Harry is too full of adrenaline to sit still for medical attention. (GF, Ch. 20)

Advisability - Wisdom. Leanne's argument with Katie Bell about the advisability of transporting strange objects *culminated* in a tussle on their way to Hogwarts. (HBP, Ch. 12)

Advised - Informed or recommended. A Ministry of Magic leaflet says, "You are advised not to leave the house alone." (HBP, Ch. 3)

Aerodynamic - Flies easily through the air. The Firebolt is described as "*honed* to aerodynamic perfection." (PA, Ch. 4)

Affronted - Insulted. Nearly Headless Nick is affronted when Ron suggests that he is afraid of the Bloody Baron. (OP, Ch. 11) Ron is affronted when a healer in a portrait at St. Mungo's sees Ron's freckles and declares that he must have a bad case of a *grievous* skin sickness called "spattergroit." (OP, Ch. 23) Ludo Bagman looks almost affronted when Harry declines his help in solving the puzzle of the egg. (GF, Ch. 24) Nearly Headless Nick is affronted when Ron says it makes no sense for a ghost to use the phrase, "I would rather die than betray his trust." (HBP, Ch. 8)

Afoul of - In conflict with. Dumbledore says Umbridge ran afoul of centaurs at Hogwarts. (HBP, Ch. 4)

Aggravated - Irritated. Harry is aggravated by Hermione's expression when she learns of the notations by the Half-Blood Prince and asks if she thinks he's cheating. (HBP, Ch. 9)

Aggravating - Frustrating or irritating. Harry finds spells used on a giant spider are aggravating to it. (GF, Ch. 31)

Aggrieved - Troubled, distressed. After mentioning Harry Potter to the Prime Minister, Cornelius Fudge settled into an aggrieved silence. (HBP, Ch. 1) After being poked by Dumbledore, Horace Slughorn rubs his belly and looks aggrieved. (HBP, Ch. 4)

Aghast - Horrified. Hermione looks aghast when Harry accuses her of sharing Ron's opinion that he "plays the hero" too much. (OP, Ch. 32)

Agitated - Disturbed, shaken up. *The Daily Prophet* quotes an agitated Ministry of Magic employee as saying he was not authorized to speak about rumors that Voldemort had returned. (HBP, Ch. 3) Slughorn looks agitated when Dumbledore suddenly announces that he and Harry will leave. (HBP, Ch. 4) Harry had never seen Dumbledore so agitated as when the headmaster tried to explain that some of Voldemort's powers transferred to Harry when Voldemort attacked him as a baby. (HBP, Ch. 23)

Agitation - State of being upset. A potion called the *Draught* of Peace soothes agitation. (OP, Ch.12) Hermione is a state of agitation after one of Fred and George's inventions punches her in the face. (HBP, Ch. 5)

Agog - Stunned. Parvati Patil is agog when Hermione tells her she is going out with Cormac McLaggen. (HBP, Ch. 15)

Airborne - Flying. Peeves is described as "a grinning, airborne *menace* who lived to cause *havoc* and distress." (CS, Ch. 8)

Airily - Lightly, in an unconcerned way. When Harry asks Dumbledore what his private lessons would concern, the headmasters says airily, "Oh, a little of this, a little of that." (HBP, Ch. 4)

Alight - Lit up. In the Mirror of Erised, Harry sees his mother alight with happiness. (PA, Ch. 11) Ron's eyes are alight with interest when discussing a conflict between Snape and Moody. (GF, Ch. 26)

Allegiance - Loyalty. Bellatrix LeStrange asks Snape whether Dumbledore has any suspicions about his true allegiance and asks, "He trusts you *implicitly* still?" (HBP, Ch. 2)

Alleging - Claiming. Rita Skeeter writes that a Ministry of Magic official (Mr. Weasley) had been alleging that no one was hurt after the appearance of the Dark Mark. (GF, Ch.10)

Allusions - Indirect references. *The Daily Prophet* prints *snide* allusions to Harry. (OP, Ch. 14)

Ally - Someone on the same side of a war or dispute; a friend. Snape says the Dark Lord dared not ask him, a former ally, for help because he did such a good job pretending to be loyal to Dumbledore. (HBP, Ch. 2)

Alternately - Taking turns, changing from one to another. While shut up in his room on Privet Drive, Harry alternately felt restless and filled with *lethargy*. (OP, Ch. 3)

Amiably - In a friendly, agreeable way. Dumbledore amiably tells Karkaroff that even he doesn't know many of Hogwarts' secrets and illustrates his point by saying he discovered a mysterious room full of *chamber pots* only that morning. (GF, Ch. 23)

Amok - In a wild, frenzied manner that puts others in danger. After Percy accuses Winky of running amok with a wand, Hermione defends her. (GF, Ch. 9)

Anecdotes - Little stories. Slughorn is full of anecdotes about *illustrious* wizards he has known. (HBP, Ch. 7)

Anguished - Troubled. Moaning Myrtle says she knows people call her fat, ugly, and miserable, then bursts into anguished sobs when Peeves says, "You've forgotten pimply." (CS, Ch. 8)

Animatedly - With interest and enthusiasm. The sight of Cho Chang chatting animatedly with another Quidditch player gave Harry a twinge of jealousy. (OP, Ch. 30)

Animosity - Dislike. Harry notices that Snape seemed strangely *wary* of displaying *overt* animosity to Mad-Eye Moody. (GF, Ch. 14)

Anonymously - With one's name and identity hidden. Ron reminds Harry that Dumbledore sent him the invisibility cloak anonymously and suggests that perhaps he sent the Firebolt, too. (PA, Ch. 11).

Apathetic - Not caring about anything. During his apathetic moods, Harry just stared at the ceiling of his room on Privet Drive. (OP, Ch. 3)

Apoplectic - Behaving oddly, as if suffering from a sudden loss of the ability to control one's body. When Aunt Marge is blown up by Harry, she makes "apoplectic popping noises." (PA, Ch. 2)

Apothecary - An old-fashioned drugstore. In Diagon Alley, Harry visits the Apothecary to buy potions ingredients. (SS, Ch. 5)

Appalled - Shocked and disgusted. When Prof. Dumbledore announces that there shall be no Quidditch Cup at Hogwarts, Fred and George are appalled. (GF, Ch. 12)

Appalling - Awful, shocking. Dumbledore says the Dursleys have inflicted appalling damage on Dudley. (HBP, Ch. 3)

Apparition - A ghost. Prof. Trelawney wonders if Harry has seen an apparition. (GF, Ch. 29)

Appeal - Request for a court or other form of authority to stop a person from being jailed or otherwise punished. Buckbeak's appeal is heard by the Committee for the Disposal of Dangerous Creatures, with an *executioner* standing by. (PA, Ch. 16)

Apportioning - Dividing up. Snape starts to criticize Lucius Malfoy but stops, saying there is no sense in apportioning blame. (HBP, Ch. 2)

Appraising - Evaluating, sizing up. After Fred Weasley asked Angelina to go to the Yule Ball, she gave him an appraising look and then said, "All right, then." (GF, Ch. 22)

Appreciatively - With thankfulness. Ron appreciatively notes his father's role in arranging transportation to Hogwarts in Ministry of Magic cars. (HBP, Ch. 6)

Apprehended - Caught. After the appearance of the Dark Mark, the *culprits* were not apprehended, according to *The Daily Prophet*. (GF, Ch. 10)

Apprehension - State of worry or anxiety. Harry, hidden in his invisibility cloak, waits with apprehension as Filch comes down the staircase toward him. (GF, Ch. 25)

Apprehensively - In a state of worry or anxiety. When Mad-Eye Moody gives instructions on what to do if one of their traveling party is killed, Harry asks apprehensively, "Is that likely?" (OP, Ch. 3)

Arachnid - Spider. Slughorn mourns Aragog at the giant spider's funeral by calling him "king of arachnids." (HBP, Ch. 22)

Argumentative - Tending to dispute other's views. Harry tried *valiantly* not to sound argumentative when discussing his destiny with Dumbledore. (HBP, Ch. 23)

Arrogant - Acting as if one is better than or knows more than others; excessively proud. Snape tells Harry that he is just like his father: "He too was exceedingly arrogant." (PA, Ch. 14)

Artifact - A hand-made object representing a culture. Dumbledore says that Voldemort would favor using artifacts with magical histories to make Horcruxes. (HBP, Ch. 23)

Ascent - Rise. Dumbledore says the years of Voldemort's ascent to power were marked by the disappearances of many witches and wizards. (GF, Ch. 30)

Ascertain - Determine. After he fights off two dementors, Harry is annoyed that all Sirius and Mr. Weasley want to do is ascertain how much damage was done. (OP, Ch. 2)

Ashen-faced - Pale. Third years sat ashen-faced after their Transfiguration class, *bemoaning* the difficulty of their homework. (PA, Ch. 16)

Askance - With suspicion or disapproval. Madam Rosmerta looks askance at Moody because he drinks from a hip flask rather than buy drink from her. (GF, Ch. 19)

Askew - Off kilter. Peeves knocked Harry's glasses askew as a prank, then sounded the alarm when he noticed the petrified forms of Justin Fitch-Fletchly and Nearly Headless Nick. (CS, Ch. 11) Harry slept with his glasses askew, snoring loudly and leaving a misty *fug* on the window. (HBP, Ch. 3)

Asperity - Harshness. When Ron asks Hermione how she can recall what people say so well, she replies, with a bit of asperity, "I listen, Ron." (OP, Ch. 12)

Aspersions - Highly critical comments, especially on someone's character. Harry never had any trouble *disbelieving* Snapes aspersions about his father until he witnessed his father's behavior in Snape's pensieve. (OP, Ch. 28)

Assent - Agreement. There is a murmur of assent after Mad-Eye Moody asks whether his class had already studied Dark creatures such as boggarts, grindylows and werewolves. (GF, Ch. 14) There is a murmur of assent from DA members after Hermione suggests that everyone carry coins that could be used to communicate. (OP, Ch. 19)

Assiduously - Diligently. With a high level of effort and attention. Voldemort assiduously seeks to learn how to destroy Harry. (OP, Ch. 37)

Assured - Said confidently. After Mrs. Norris was petrified, Ron assured Ginny that such events don't happen often at Hogwarts and the *maniac* will soon be caught. (CS, Ch. 9) [compare to *"ensure"*]

Astray - Off course. Harry is afraid his reply to Dumbledore may have gone astray. (HBP, Ch. 3)

Asylum - Hospital for the mentally ill. The young Tom Riddle fears Dumbledore has come to take him to an asylum. (HBP, Ch. 13)

Atmosphere - Feeling of a place. Near the end of Dumbledore's visit to Privet Drive, Harry senses the atmosphere is so uncomfortable for the Dursleys that it is "thick like cold custard." (HBP, Ch. 3)

Atrocity - Terrible, wicked event. The Prime Minister tells Cornelius Fudge that he would have tried to catch Voldemort before he committed the atrocity of destroying the Brockdale Bridge. (HBP, Ch. 1)

Attendant - Accompanying. Dumbledore says Merope's experience with *unrequited* love and the attendant despair may have sapped her powers. (HBP, Ch. 13)

Audible - Able to be heard. When Voldemort tells Frank Bryce, "I am not a man" but something "much, much worse," his voice is barely audible. (GF, Ch. 1) Ron's voice is barely audible when he mumbles about his relationship with Hermione. (HBP, Ch. 15)

Augury - An omen. Ron tries to write "augury" in an essay but his spell-check pen malfunctions. (HBP, Ch. 21)

Aura - An air or field of energy that surrounds a person. Luna Lovegood projects "an aura of distinct dottiness." (OP, Ch. 10) Prof. Trelawney tells Hermione, "I see very little aura around you." (PA, Ch. 6).

Austere - Stern. At his hearing, members of the Wizengamot look at Harry with austere expressions. (OP, Ch. 8) Mrs. Weasley seems *flustered* with the austere manner of the Aurors *escorting* Harry and her children to Kings Cross Station. (HBP, Ch. 7)

Averted - Turned away as to avoid. While Harry begs Prof. McGonagall to let him have the Firebolt back, Hermione (who alerted the Prof. about the *anonymous* gift) hurries past with her eyes averted. (PA, Ch. 11)

Avidly - With great interest. Harry noticed that the members of the Order of the Phoenix were gazing at him avidly, and he felt embarrassed that he had not combed his hair in four days. (OP, Ch. 3) Harry notices Kreacher staring at him avidly, making Harry *vaguely* suspicious. (OP, Ch. 24)

Awestruck - Stunned, impressed. When Winky meets Harry for the first time, she looks awestruck. (GF, Ch. 8) Ron is awestruck that Hagrid walked into a camp of giants. (OP, Ch. 20)

Awkwardly - In an unstable and clumsy way. Harry sees Molly Weasley's magic clock perched awkwardly atop a load of laundry. (HBP, Ch. 5)

Badgering - Nagging. After Harry and Ron buy SPEW badges from Hermione, they find her badgering them to wear them and to persuade others to do the same. (GF, Ch. 15)

Baffling - Unable to be understood. The Prime Minister tells Fudge that the murder of Amelia Bones was *baffling* to Muggle police and had been getting a lot of *publicity*. (HBP, Ch. 1)

Balaclava - A knit hat covering the head and neck. In winter, Hagrid wears a balaclava. (CS, Ch. 11)

Balderdash - Nonsense. Balderdash was one of the passwords to get into the Gryffindor common room. (GF, Ch. 21)

Balefully - In sinister or threatening way, such as a giving someone a dirty look. Slughorn looks at Dumbledore balefully when the headmaster suggests Death Eaters would be interested in recruiting him. (HBP, Ch. 4)

Ballistic - Like a bullet. Ron warns that his mother is "going ballistic" - that is, about to explode. (OP, Ch. 10)

Bandy-legged - Bowlegged. In Hogsmeade Harry sees a bandy-legged man he soon recognizes as Mundungus Fletcher. (HBP, Ch. 12)

Banish - Order to stay away. Prof. Trelawney asks Dumbledore to banish "the *usurping* nag" — Firenze. (HBP, Ch. 20)

Barking - In England, crazy. After Ron and Harry make up after a long period of not talking to each other, Hermione bursts into tears, and Ron calls her "barking mad." (GF, Ch. 20)

Barmy - In England, silly or weird. Dobby learns that he is free to call Dumbledore a barmy old codger if he wants because having the ability to speak one's mind is part of being free. (GF, Ch. 21)

Beckoned - Waved, in a way to ask someone to come or follow. Wood, unable to come up with a pre-game speech, just beckons to the Gryffindor team to follow him to the Quidditch *pitch*. (PA, Ch. 9)

Bedecked - Decorated with. Harry notices that none of the Bulgarian tents at the Quidditch World Cup are bedecked with flowers, but all display a poster of Victor Krum. (GF, Ch. 7)

Bedraggled - Wet and limp, like someone after being caught in a sudden rainstorm. After Peeves unleashes water balloons on unsuspecting students, Prof. McGonagall instructs the bedraggled crowd to go into the Great Hall. (GF, Ch. 12)

Befits - Is appropriate. After Harry asks Kreacher what Malfoy is up to, Kreather says Draco moves with "a nobility that befits his pure blood." (HBP, Ch. 21)

Befouled - Made dirty. When Madam Pince sees the markings in Harry's potions text, she angrily describes the marked-up book as *despoiled*, *desecrated* and befouled. (HBP, Ch. 15)

Befouling - Making dirty. After Harry tracks mud inside the Hogwarts castle, Filch fills out a form saying he has broken a rule by "befouling the castle." (CS, Ch. 8)

Befuddled - Lost the ability to think clearly, usually due to consuming too much food or drink. Dumbledore announces in the Great Hall that he has something serious to say "before you become befuddled by our excellent feast." (PA, Ch. 5).

Belligerent - Hostile, quarrelsome. Ron tries to write "belligerent" in an essay but his spell-check pen malfunctions. (HBP, Ch. 21)

Bemoaning - Complaining about. Third years sat *ashen-faced*, bemoaning the difficulty of their homework. (PA, Ch. 16)

Bemused - Bewildered. Ron shook his head, bemused, after Luna Lovegood made an odd comment about how she would have felt being Ron's companion at a dance. (OP, Ch. 10)

Benignly - Harmlessly, unthreateningly. Dolores Umbridge smiled benignly as Dumbledore explained how had he had arranged for Sibyll Trelawney to stay at Hogwarts. (OP, Ch. 26)

Benumbed - Made numb. Harry feels rock faces with benumbed fingers after swimming in icy water with Dumbledore. (HBP, Ch. 26)

Berk - In England, a stupid person. Sirius says that when they were young, he and James Potter were sometimes *arrogant* berks. (OP, Ch. 29)

Berserk - Wild, crazy, dangerous. "Hey Potter," Malfoy taunts. "You feeling all right? You're not going to go berserk on us?" (GF, Ch. 31)

Berth - A place, or, when used with the word "wide," a safe distance. Harry avoids even going near the bathroom in which Moaning Myrtle lives by giving it a wide berth. (HBP, Ch. 21)

Beseechingly - In a way that conveys a desperate need for help. Narcissa Malfoy looks at Snape beseechingly when she asks him to protect Draco. (HBP, Ch. 2)

Besieged - Faced with many. Harry finds himself besieged with requests to give a firsthand *account* of how Dumbledore came to leave Hogwarts and leave Dolores Umbridge in charge. (OP, Ch. 28)

Besmirch - Make dirty. When Harry says "Voldemort," Bellatrix Lestrange accuses him of besmirching the Dark Lord's name by speaking it with "unworthy lips." (OP, Ch. 35)

Besotted - Unable to think clearly, usually because of drunkenness. Dumbledore guesses that Merope was so besotted by love for Tom Riddle Sr. that she perhaps believed he had come to love her, too. (HBP, Ch. 10) Dumbledore describes Hepzibah as besotted. (HBP, Ch. 20)

Bespectacled - Wearing glasses. Harry is a skinny, black-haired, bespectacled boy. (OP, Ch. 1)

Bestial - Brutal, like a beast's passion. When Tom Riddle learns he is a wizard, his face shows not pleasure but a rough expression that is almost bestial. (HBP, Ch. 13)

Bestows - Gives. After claiming that Harry is dating Hermione, Rita Skeeter writes that Harry's well-wishers must hope that next time he "bestows his heart on a *worthier* candidate." (GF, Ch. 27)

Betray - Reveal. The Prime Minister, also known as "Minister of Muggles," tries not to let his face betray any surprise when Fudge emerges from the fireplace in his office. (HBP, Ch. 1)

Bewildered - Confused. While transformed into Goyle by polyjuice potion, Harry looks bewildered when Hermione says she won't leave her bathroom stall. (CS, Ch. 12) Harry is bewildered when he mentions breathing to Moaning Myrtle, and her eyes promptly fill with tears. (GF, Ch. 25)

Bigheaded - Thinking a lot of one's self. Gilderoy Lockhart *paternally* advises Harry that handing out signed pictures can look a *tad* bigheaded. (CS, Ch. 6)

Bigotry - Not liking anyone who does not share one's background or beliefs. Hermione thinks all the *hysteria* over giants is just *prejudice* and bigotry. (GF, Ch. 24)

Bilge - Worthless ideas. When Dumbledore says that he believes the dementors are talking orders from someone other than Ministry of Magic officials, Fudge dismisses this as bilge. (OP, Ch. 8)

Binding - Unable to be broken. Placing one's name in the Goblet of Fire *constitutes* a binding contract. (GF, Ch. 16)

Blackmail - Threatening to reveal information or take an unwanted action unless one's demands are met. When arguing about whether the destruction of the Brockdale Bridge could have been prevented, Cornelius Fudge says he could not give in to Lord Voldemort's blackmail. (HBP, Ch. 1)

Blanched - Turned white with dismay. Ginny Weasley blanched when Ron said he hoped the *maniac* terrorizing Hogwarts would petrify Filch before he's caught. (CS, Ch. 9)

Blancmange - A sweet food made from flour, sugar and milk. Ron notices this unfamiliar dessert while the girls from Beaubatons are visiting. (GF, Ch. 16)

Blandly - In a dull, lifeless way. After caught by Umbridge after a meeting of the D.A., Harry answers Cornelius Fudge's questions blandly. (OP, Ch. 27)

Blankly - In a dazed or confused way. Harry stares blankly when told that Dobby wants to be paid for his work, not understanding that this is an unusual idea for a house elf. (GF, Ch. 8)

Blatant - Obvious. Despite orders to behave like Muggles, there were blatant signs of magic at the Quidditch World Cup site. (GF, Ch. 7) A figure in a portrait complains of blatant corruption when it becomes clear that Willy Widdershins was not prosecuted for making Muggle toilets *regurgitate* because he was an informant for Umbridge about Harry's activities. (OP, Ch. 27) Harry thinks that the reason Mr. Dursley says nothing to Dumbledore is that he is shocked by the "blatant wizardishness" of his appearance. (HBP, Ch. 3)

Blighter - In England, a person held in low esteem. At the Quidditch World Cup, Fudge complains that "these Bulgarian blighters have been trying to *cadge* all the best places." (GF, Ch. 8)

Blimey - In England, an exclamation like "yikes." Ron says this when he and Harry find a snakeskin that's 20 feet long in the Chamber of Secrets. (CS, Ch. 16)

Blinkered - Of limited vision, like a racehorse fitted with a hood that keeps its eyes looking forward. Firenze says Sybill Trelawney may have some talent, but that, like all humans, she is blinkered and *fettered* "by the limitations of her kind." (OP, Ch. 27)

Blithely - Without care or concern. Harry announces it's time for a Quidditch match blithely. (HBP, Ch. 14)

Bloke - In England, a fellow. Ron asks, "Is Lockhart the *smarmiest* bloke you've ever met, or what?" (CS, Ch. 13)

Bloodshed - Violence involving the loss of life. In Defense Against the Dark Arts, students learn that Red Caps lurk wherever there is bloodshed. (PA, Ch. 8)

Bloodshot - Red-streaked; used to describe the eyes of person who is drunk, tired or ill. Kreacher has bloodshot eyes. (HBP, Ch. 3)

Bloodthirsty - Violent; eager to harm. Rita Skeeter describes the race of giants as bloodthirsty and brutal. (GF, Ch. 24)

Bludgeon - To hit with a heavy object. In Defense Against the Dark Arts, students learn that Red Caps like to bludgeon people on deserted battlefields. (PA, Ch. 8)

Blundered - Moved unsteadily. Harry blundered up the hall in anger after Ernie McMillan accused him of telling a snake to attack Justin Finch-Fletchley. (CS, Ch. 11)

Blunders (verb) - Makes a huge mistake. "Ministry blunders" is the headline in *The Daily Prophet* after the appearance of the Dark Mark at the Quidditch World Cup, because the *culprits* were not *apprehended*. (GF, Ch. 10)

Blustering - Windy or full of wordiness. Harry perceives Fudge as *pompous* and blustering, but he seems angry and unable to face reality after Voldemort returns. (GF, Ch. 36)

Boded - Indicated by a sign or clue. After noticing that Cornelius Fudge looks worn and worried, the Prime Minister recalls that whenever he had seen such a look in a politician, it never boded well. (HBP, Ch. 1)

Boisterous - Loud, laughing and rowdy. Peeves is boisterous. (PA, Ch. 20) Uncle Vernon describes Dudley as boisterous but adds, "he wouldn't hurt a fly!" (GF, Ch. 3)

Bout - Brief period of activity. Harry is filled with guilt when thinks about the bout of rule-breaking he and Ron are planning. (CS, Ch. 12)

Bracingly - In a manner to provide energy and support. Ron bracingly tells Ginny, a cat-lover, that she would not be so concerned about Mrs. Norris being petrified if she knew the cat well. (CS, Ch. 9)

Braggart - Person who boasts. Sir Cadogan calls Harry a "scurvy braggart" until he understands that Harry is not making fun of him but merely lost. (PA, Ch. 6)

Brambles - A prickly shrub. Following the spiders, Harry and Ron deal with branches and brambles. (CS, Ch. 15)

Brandishing - Waving something, usually in a way to threaten or impress. There is a lot of brandishing in the Harry Potter books: Madame Pince the librarian brandishes a feather duster to insist Harry leave the library (SS, Ch. 12); Sir Cadogan brandishes his sword before he understands that Harry, Ron and Hermione have not come to laugh at him but need his help (PA, Ch. 6); Frank Bryce brandishes a stick at boys that trespass on the Riddle family property (GF, Ch. 1); Uncle Vernon brandishes a letter from Mrs. Weasley (GF, Ch. 3); A ministry wizard brandishes a pair of pinstriped pants at a wizard who was walking around in a flowery nightgown (GF, Ch. 7); Sirius Black brandishes a chicken leg while asking questions about Barty Crouch (GF, Ch. 27); In her portrait, Sirius Black's mother brandishes clawed hands as if to scratch the faces of Lupin and Mrs. Weasley (OP, Ch. 4); Hagrid brandishes his fists (OP, Ch. 31); Harry sees Morfin brandishing a wand in one hand and a knife in the other (HBP, Ch. 10); Quidditch fans can be seen brandishing banners and scarves. (HBP, Ch. 24)

Bravado - A swaggering manner used by someone pretending to be more brave that he or she is. Ron speaks with bravado after Hermione and Harry discover him in a room with Lavender Brown. (HBP, Ch. 14)

Breach - Break. Harry understands that the Dursleys are upset about the Dementors turning up in Little Whinging because the event represents a breach in a great, invisible wall that divides the wizarding world and the Muggle world. (OP, Ch. 2) While taking an OWL in History of Magic, Harry puzzles over a question about how the Statute of Secrecy was breached in 1749. (OP, Ch. 31)

Breathlessly - In an excited way, breathing rapidly. Hermione asks Harry breathlessly whether he and Ron have bits of Crabbe and Goyle for the Polyjuice Potion. (CS, Ch. 12)

Brightly - Happily. When Harry lies to Neville, saying he needs to go to the library, Neville says brightly, "I'll come with you!" (PA, Ch. 14)

Brimming - Flowing over. When Harry comes to see Dobby, Dobby's eyes are brimming with tears of happiness. (GF, Ch.21)

Broodingly - In a troubled, thoughtful mood. Ron stares broodingly at the Acid Pops in Honeydukes, remembering when one burnt a hole in his tongue when he was seven. (PA, Ch. 10)

Brow - Forehead. Mr. Weasley reads *The Daily Prophet* with a *furrowed* brow. (PA, Ch. 5)

Brusquely - Bluntly, harshly. When Umbridge demands to know how many years she has been teaching at Hogwarts, Prof. McGonagall answers brusquely. (OP, Ch. 15) Harry tells Ginny brusquely that it's not Cho he wants to talk to, but Sirius. (OP, Ch. 29) Phineaus Nigellus brusquely says he doesn't believe the news that Sirius is dead. (OP, Ch. 36)

Budgerigars - Parakeets. See entry for *Budgie*, below.

Budgie - A parakeet. The Muggle news features a waterskiing budgie named Bungy the Budgie. (OP, Ch. 1)

Bulbous - Round (most often used to describe someone's nose). Filch has a bulbous nose. (CS, Ch. 8) Winky has a bulbous nose. (GF, Ch. 9)

Buoyant - Cheerful. After the Quidditch World Cup, Ludo Bagman *emerges* from some trees, and Harry notices that he no longer looks buoyant and rosy-faced. (GF, Ch. 9)

Burgeoned - Grew. A spark of hope burgeoned in Harry's chest that he might not be expelled from Hogwarts, after all. (OP, Ch. 2)

Burnished - Made shiny by polishing. Grigotts Banks has burnished bronze doors. (SS, Ch. 5)

Cackling - Laughing. Harry sees a group of goblins cackling over a sack of gold they had apparently won by betting on the Quidditch World Cup; he notices they seem quite *unperturbed* by nearby noise and flashes of light. (GF, Ch. 9)

Cadge - To get something without paying for it. At the Quidditch World Cup, Fudge complains that "these Bulgarian *blighters* have been trying to cadge all the best places." (GF, Ch. 8)

Cajolingly - In way to persuade. When the flying car begins to lose speed, Ron shakes the steering wheel cajolingly and says, "Come on." (CS, Ch. 5)

Calamity - Awful event. Prof. Trelawney has habit of predicting calamity. (HBP, Ch. 25)

Caliber - Quality. Slughorn tells Tom Riddle that wizards of a certain caliber have always been curious about the dark arts. (HBP, Ch. 23)

Callously - In an uncaring way. Umbridge callously tells Prof. Trelawney that she should have seen it coming that she would be booted out of Hogwarts. (OP, Ch. 26)

Campaign - Organized effort. Rita Skeeter writes that Hagrid plans to continue a campaign of *intimidation* by forcing students to care for blast-ended skrewts. (GF, Ch. 24)

Canopy - Covering. The flying car dives beneath a canopy of clouds to keep track of the route of the Hogwarts Express. (CS, Ch. 5) Harry sleeps in a four-poster bed beneath a canopy. (CS, Ch. 7)

Caress - Tender touch. When Snape talks of the Dark Arts, Harry hears a loving caress in his voice. (HBP, Ch. 9)

Careworn - Worried. When the Prime Minister sees Cornelius Fudge, he notices that Fudge looks careworn. (HBP, Ch. 1) After discussing Fleur Delacour's engagement to Bill Weasley, Mrs. Weasley leaves the room looking careworn. (HBP, Ch. 5)

Casually - Calmly, as if everything is quite normal. Harry casually mentions to Uncle Vernon that he is touch with Sirius Black, who might be concerned if he doesn't hear from Harry for a while. (GF, Ch. 3)

Cavernous - Like a huge cave. Hogwarts' entrance hall is cavernous. (PA, Ch. 5).

Cavort - Play. Moody complains that former Death Eaters cavorted at the Quidditch Cup but fled when he sent the Dark Mark into the sky. (GF, Ch. 35)

Chamber pot - Container that people used to relieve themselves before flush toilets were invented. Dumbledore tells about discovering a room full of chamber pots that he thinks may be accessible only at 5:30 a.m., or when the moon is quarter-full, or when the seeker "has an exceptionally full bladder." (GF, Ch. 23)

Channeling - Speaking on behalf of the spirit of a dead person. When Angelina speaks fiercely to Harry about the importance of attending Quidditch practice, Harry tells Ron, "I think we'd better check with Puddlemore United whether Oliver Wood's been killed during a training session, because she seems to be channeling his spirit." (OP, Ch. 13)

Cheek - Disrespect. After Harry suggests in his first potions class that Snape call on Hermione instead of badgering him, Snape deducts a house point from Gryffindor for "your cheek." (SS, Ch. 8)

Cherished - Kept in mind fondly, adored. Merope cherished Tom Riddle, Sr. (HBP, Ch. 10)

Chilling - Scary. Ron's tale of how he awoke and saw Sirius Black standing over him with a knife was chilling. (PA, Ch. 14)

Chivalry - Willingness to fight to protect the weak and uphold justice, like knights during the Middle Ages. The Sorting Hat sings of Gryffindors' "daring, nerve and chivalry." (SS, Ch. 7)

Chivvying - Moving in small steps. Harry found Tonks chivvying him down the steps out of 12 Grimmauld Place. (OP, Ch. 24)

Chortled - Laughed in a gleeful way. Sir Headless Nick chortled when Hermione asks if house elves get sick leave and pensions. (GF, Ch. 12)

Christened - Named. Hagrid loves dangerous animals so much that he christened a giant, three-headed dog with the name "Fluffy." (CS, Ch. 14)

Chuffed - In England, satisfied. In deciding where to practice defensive spells, Harry says that he can't imagine Madam Pince being too chuffed if they started casting jinxes and counter-jinxes in the library. (OP, Ch. 16)

Chunter - In England, to mutter. Ron is so upset that Ginny is dating Michael Corner that he chunters and utters *imprecations* under his breath. (OP, Ch. 16)

Churlish - Ill-tempered and hard to work with. After a student compliments Harry, he says, "Yeah, well ..." because he thought it would be churlish to disagree. (OP, Ch. 15)

Cinders - Ashes. If you fail to open a Howler quickly, Percy says, the explosion can reduce whatever is on your desk to cinders. (GF, Ch. 10)

Circulating - Going around. Snape reminds Bellatrix LeStrange that when Harry Potter first came to Hogwarts, there were lots of rumors circulating, including whispers that he might be a dark wizard. (HBP, Ch. 2)

Civil - Polite. Uncle Vernon warns Harry that he must speak to Aunt Marge with a "civil tongue." (PA, Ch. 2)

Clambered - Moved awkwardly. Neville clambered down the ladder from the Divination classroom. (PA, Ch. 16)

Clammy - Moist and uncomfortable. Fleur Delacour looked pale and clammy before facing her dragon in the Tri-Wizard Tournament. (GF, Ch. 20)

Clamoring - Demanding. After the Dark Mark appears, the keeper of the Portkeys has to deal with many wizards clamoring for access to a Portkey. (GF, Ch. 10)

Clarified - Made clear. Dumbledore tells Harry that the Order of the Phoenix has vacated 12 Grimmauld Place under several issues involving enchantments on the house can be clarified. (HBP, Ch. 3)

Clenched - Held tightly. When Dobby disapparates, Harry finds his fist clenched on thin air. (CS, Ch. 10) Through clenched teeth, Harry informs Uncle Vernon, "You can't give a dementor the old one-two." (OP, Ch. 2)

Cloistered - Kept apart from others, as if in a monastery. Harry thinks about Ron and Hermione being cloistered in the prefect's carriage as he looks for a place to sit on the Hogwarts Express. (HBP, Ch. 7)

Clutch - A group of eggs or chickens. When Harry sees his Hungarian Horntail during the Triwizard Tournament, she is crouched low over her clutch of eggs. (GF, Ch. 20)

Cobbled - Paved with stones. Diagon Alley is described as cobbled. (PA, Ch. 4)

Codswallop - In England, nonsense. Hagrid says that claims that Voldemort is gone forever are codswallop, in his opinion. (SS, Ch.4)

Coercion - Action of forcing people to do something. Dumbledore suspects the Death Eaters would love to have Slughorn use his *considerable* talents for coercion, torture and murder. (HBP, Ch. 4)

Cogs - Clock parts; also, what one might imagine to find turning inside the brain of someone who is thinking hard. Harry can almost see the cogs working inside Uncle Vernon's head as he decides he would rather let Harry go to the Quidditch World Cup than risk a visit from Sirius Black. (GF, Ch. 3)

Coincided - Happened at the same time or place. Harry noticed that Ron's hostile attitude coincided with a decline in his skills as keeper in Quidditch. (HBP, Ch. 14)

Colleague - Co-worker. The Ministry of Magic issues a *pamphlet* that explains what to do if a friend, colleague or family member appears to be acting strangely. (HBP, Ch. 3)

Collective - Group. When Sirius says Voldemort's name, there is a collective shudder around the table. (OP, Ch. 5) While Viktor Krum was fighting his Chinese Fireball, Harry hears the crowd draw a collective breath. (GF, Ch. 20)

Colossal - Huge. After the curse Mosmordre is spoken, a colossal skull appears in the sky. (GF, Ch. 9)

Colluding - Working together for an evil purpose. Hermione says wizards are colluding in the *oppression* of house elves. (GF, Ch. 15)

Collywobbles - In England, a feeling of worry and discomfort. Dementors give even Hagrid the collywobbles. (PA, Ch. 3)

Comeuppance - Well-deserved punishment. Harry hopes Draco will get his comeuppance after Hermione completes the Polyjuice Potion. (CS, Ch. 12) Hermione says that if Barty Crouch looks ill, it's just his comeuppance for *sacking* Winky. (GF, Ch. 27)

Commending - Applauding, praising. Prof. Trelawney reads portions of students' predictions about their future, commending them for their *unflinching* acceptance of the horrors that await them. (GF, Ch. 15)

Commiserating - Suffering together in a sympathetic way. After Harry's decision to save two people cost him a first-place finish in the one of the tasks in Triwizard competition, Ron and Hermione give him "half-*exasperated*, half-commiserating looks." (GF, Ch. 26) After serving a detention during a Quidditch match, Harry wonders if he will find his teammates celebrating or commiserating. (HBP, Ch. 24)

Commotion - Frenzied activity. There is commotion in The Burrow as everyone struggles to get ready to leave for King's Cross. (OP, Ch. 10) Harry hears muffled commotion in the hallway, which turns out to be Prof. Trelawney screaming as Umbridge. (OP, Ch. 26) Prof. Trelawney tells Harry that she heard a commotion in the hall during her job interview (during which she made a prediction about Voldemort) and that the door flew open to reveal Severus Snape. (HBP, Ch. 25)

Compelled - Forced or driven to do something. Draco Malfoy appears compelled to converse with Dumbledore despite his orders just to kill him. (HBP, Ch. 27)

Compere - In England, a master of ceremonies. Slughorn acts like a compere introducing acts in the first meeting of the Slug Club. (HBP, Ch. 7)

Complacently - In an unconcerned way. Fleur Delacour speaks complacently about the exam results that Hermione frets over. (HBP, Ch. 5)

Complementary - Going together well. Mr. Weasley receives the Muggle remedy of stitches from a wizard doctor who is interested in finding Muggle techniques that are complementary with wizard medicine. (OP, Ch. 23)

Complied - Followed a request or rule. Barty Crouch complies with the instruction to dress like a Muggle so well that Harry thinks that he could pass for a bank manager. (GF, Ch. 7)

Composedly - Calmly. Hermonie speaks composedly when thinking about what she should buy for herself. Ron suggests, sarcastically, "How about a nice *book*." (PA, Ch. 4)

Comprehension - Understanding. When Harry mentions Lord Voldemort, Uncle Vernon's face shows comprehension that this was the same wizard who had killed Harry's parents. (OP, Ch. 2) Snape's face shows an expression of *dawning* comprehension when he sees the Marauder's Map lying on the staircase, near an egg belonging to a Triwizard champion. (GF, Ch. 25)

Compressed - Squeezed. When apparating with Dumbledore, Harry feels as if he is being compressed beyond *endurance*. (HBP, Ch. 25)

Comprised - Made up of. At the Quidditch World Cup, Harry sees a shimmering shamrock in the sky, which he realizes is comprised of thousands of leprechauns. (GF, Ch. 8) The Dark Mark in the sky is comprised of emerald stars. (GF, Ch. 9)

Concealed - Hidden. Harry is glad to be concealed in the bushes because Mrs. Figg has gotten in the habit of inviting him to tea every time she sees him. (OP, Ch. 1)

Conceited - Thinking a lot of oneself. Sirius tells James Potter that Lily Evans thinks he is a bit conceited. (OP, Ch. 28)

Concocted - Created from many ingredients. Lupin says that Snape has concocted a potion for him. (PA, Ch. 8)

Concussed - Knocked in the head. Hermione says Pansy Parkinson is *"thicker* than a concussed troll." (OP, Ch. 10)

Condemned - Forced into a terrible fate. The Sorting Hat sings that it is condemned to split students into four houses, and it worries that this may be the wrong thing to do. (OP, Ch. 11)

Condensation - Water coming out of the air. During the winter, condensation covers the windows of the greenhouse where Herbology classes meet. (GF, Ch. 24)

Confection - A sweet food or (less commonly) an example of superb craftsmanship. One of the tents at the Quidditch World Cup is an *extravagant* "confection of striped silk." (GF, Ch. 7)

Confidentially - In a trusting way, as when sharing a secret. Dobby tells Harry confidentially that Winky is having trouble adjusting to life without serving Mr. Crouch. (GF, Ch. 21)

Confiding - Telling someone a secret. Dumbledore says Harry would do his friends a *disservice* by not confiding in them about the prophecy. (HBP, Ch. 4)

Confiscated - Taken away by an authority figure. Filch had confiscated the Marauder's Map from some unknown student and filed it in his office. (PA, Ch. 10) Dumbledore informs Harry that Fred and George sent him a toilet seat, but that Madam Pomfrey confiscated it because it was not very *hygienic*. (SS, Ch. 17)

Congealed - Turned solid. In the Room of Requirement, Harry sees congealed potions, among other things. (HBP, Ch. 24)

Congealing - To become solid after being a liquid. Harry is so distracted by Umbridge's visit to Snape's classroom that he discovers his potion is congealing into a smelly mess. (OP, Ch. 17)

Congregated - Gathered together. Harry and Ron saw a large crowd congregated around a sign that announced the arrival of students from Beaubatons and Durmstrang. (GF, Ch. 15)

Conjure - Create by magic. Mr. Weasley conjures candles to light the garden of The Burrow. (GF, Ch. 5)

Conscience - One's inner sense of right and wrong. Harry's conscience bothers him because he misled Hagrid into thinking he had made progress with his egg in the Triwizard competition. (GF, Ch. 24)

Consented - Agreed. Despite being *sacked* as Minister of Magic, Cornelius Fudge has consented to remain on as an advisor, Rufus Scrimgeour tells the Prime Minister. (HBP, Ch. 1) Hermione consented to help Harry with a paper for Herbology, which Harry interpreted as a good sign after a lot of tension between her and Ron. (HBP, Ch. 20)

Considerable - Large, impressive. Dumbledore suspects the Death Eaters would love to have Slughorn use his considerable talents for *coercion*, torture and murder. (HBP, Ch. 4)

Consolation - Comforting actions or expressions. Sirius' letters contain words of consolation. (OP, Ch. 1)

Consolingly - In a comforting way. Harry pats Hagrid's arm consolingly at Aragog's funeral. (HBP, Ch. 22)

Consorted - Hung around with. Dumbledore says Tom Riddle consorted with "the very worst of our kind" before becoming Lord Voldemort. (CS, Ch. 18)

Conspicuous - Obvious, easily noticed. At King's Cross Station, Hogwarts students try not to be conspicuous as they enter platform nine and three-quarters. (GF, Ch. 10)

Conspiratorially - As if part of a conspiracy. Ernie McMillan conspiratorially tells Harry, Ron and Hermione that Dolores Umbridge attempted to enter the headmaster's office after Dumbledore left. (OP, Ch. 28)

Consternation - Dismay. To Harry's consternation, Ron agrees with Hermione that Harry ought to teach his fellow students about defending oneself against a dark wizard. (OP, Ch. 15)

Constitutes - Forms or creates. Placing one's name in the Goblet of Fire constitutes a *binding*, magical contract. (GF, Ch. 16) Harry is accused of performing a Patronus Charm in a Muggle-inhabited area, which Ministry of Magic officials say constitutes a violation a Decrees for the Reasonable Restriction of Underage Wizardry. (OP, Ch. 8)

Constricted - Squeezed or held to a limited space. Mr. Weasley says in a constricted voice that half of the members of his family owe their lives to Harry. (HBP, Ch. 19)

Consumed - Being caught in an emotion or *obsessed* with an idea. Harry is consumed with anger and frustration as he awaits information on what has happened in the wizarding world over the summer. (OP, Ch 3)

Contagious - Catching, like a cold or flu. When Dobby says he wants to be paid for his work and he likes being free, the other house elves edge away from him as if he had something contagious. (GF, Ch. 21)

Contaminated - Ruined by the addition of something, like drinking water contaminated with poison. After the prophecy is revealed, Harry is glad that his friends don't view him as contaminated or dangerous. (HBP, Ch. 5)

Contamination - Infection. Because the moon was not full when Fenrir Greyback bit Bill Weasley, Ron was hopeful that there might not be enough contamination to result in werewolf qualities. (HBP, Ch. 27)

Contemplated - Thought about. Umbridge contemplated Hermione's offer to go see Dumbledore's weapon, then accepted. (OP, Ch. 32)

Contemptuous - Full of disgust. While Ron is dating Lavender Brown, Hermione only stays in his presence long enough to give him a contemptuous look. (HBP, Ch. 18)

Contemptuously - With disgust. Stan speaks contemptuously when he notes how unobservant Muggles are. (PA, Ch. 3)

Contorted - Twisted unnaturally. Snape's face is contorted with anger when he shows Lupin the enchanted piece of parchment that Harry had in his pocket. (PA, Ch. 14) Victor Krum's face is contorted with concentration as he pulls out of dangerous dive during the Quidditch World Cup. (GF, Ch. 8) Madam Pince's face is contorted when she discovers Harry eating a chocolate Easter egg in the library. (OP, Ch. 29) Snape personalizes his classroom by putting up *gruesome* pictures of people with strangely contorted body parts. (HBP, Ch. 9) Draco Malfoy's mouth contorts *involuntarily* when Dumbledore points out that he has had several minutes to kill him but had failed to do so. (HBP, Ch. 27)

Contradicted - Denied or implied the opposite. When Sirius said a house elf cannot leave his or her house, Harry contradicted him and recalled how Dobby left the Malfoys to visit him on Privet Drive. (OP, Ch. 23)

Contradicting - Saying the opposite. As part of the Inquisitorial Squad, Malfoy takes points away from Hufflepuff's Ernie McMillan "for contradicting me." (OP, Ch. 27)

Contrary - Against or opposite, as in "on the contrary." Draco Malfoy stops *strutting* about Hogwarts as if he owned the place after his father is *sacked* from the Hogwarts Board of Governors: "On the contrary, he looked *resentful* and *sulky*." (CS, Ch. 18) Despite what Slughorn said to the contrary, Harry though he should not have be so surprised to hear that a Muggle-born witch was highly talented. (HBP, Ch. 4)

Controversial - Considered bad by some people but good by others. Rita Skeeter reports that Dumbledore has a history of making controversial staff appointments. (GF, Ch. 24)

Conversationally - In a casual tone and manner. While Hogwarts is under attack by Death Eaters, Dumbledore conversationally tells Draco that it sounds like someone is putting up a good fight. (HBP, Ch. 27)

Converse - Speak. A parseltongue has the ability to converse with snakes. (GF, Ch. 31)

Convert - Change. After Hagrid gives Slughorn some unicorn hair, the potions professor inspects Hagrid's cabin for anything else he might be able to sell and convert into "a plentiful supply of oak-matured mead, crystallized pineapple and velvet smoking jackets." (HBP, Ch. 22)

Convey - Communicate. The Prime Minister makes it clear to Fudge that he's been having a bad week, hoping to convey that he does not want additional bad news. (HBP, Ch. 1) Snape refuses to tell Bellatrix LeStrange what information he gathered about Dumbledore, saying it has been conveyed directly to the Dark Lord. (HBP, Ch. 2)

Convulsively -With spasms of tightness. Harry gripped his wand convulsively while confronting Sirius Black. (PA, Ch. 17)

Coordinated - Working together. At the Quidditch World Cup, Harry is impressed at how coordinated the Irish players are. (GF, Ch. 8)

Copiously - In great amount. Hagrid weeps copiously at Dumbledore's funeral (HBP, Ch. 27)

Copse - Thicket of trees. With the help of the pensieve, Harry and Dumbledore follow Bob Ogden past a copse to the home of the Gaunts. (HBP, Ch. 10)

Corporeal - Having a body. The head of the Department of Magical Law Enforcement, Madam Bone, is quite impressed when she learns that Harry can produce a corporeal patronus. (OP, Ch. 8)

Corpulent - Fat. One of the portraits on the wall of the Headmaster's study is a corpulent wizard who says he misses Dumbledore. (OP, Ch. 36)

Corresponded - Wrote letters. Albus Dumbledore tells Petunia Dursley that they had corresponded, which Harry realizes was a reference to the howler that Dumbledore sent. (HBP, Ch. 3)

Correspondingly - In a matching way. Dumbledore tells Harry that he is smarter than the average person, and so his mistakes are "correspondingly huger." (HBP, Ch. 10)

Corruption - The situation in which people in government make deals to allow their friends to enjoy special privileges, such as not being punished for breaking the law. A wizard in a painting cries out, "Blatant corruption!" when he hears that a wizard escaped punishment for making Muggle toilets explode because he served as an informant to Dolores Umbridge. (OP, Ch. 27)

Cosseted - Pampered, like a pet. Harry views Slughorn's method of hiding out in Muggle homes to be a cosseted existence and cowardly compared to Sirius's willingness to live in caves and eat rats in order to fight dark wizards. (HBP, Ch. 4)

Countenance - Face. In the library, Hermione and Harry are confronted with the vulture-like countenance of Madam Pince, who told them the library was closed. (HBP, Ch. 15)

Counterpart - A person, animal or object that closely resembles or matches another. When Harry hears the crowd roar, he realizes that Cedric has come face-to-face with the life-sized counterpart of the miniature Swedish Short-Snort that he had pulled from Ludo Bagman's purple silk sack. (GF, Ch. 20)

Coursing - Running through. After he learns the story of how Sirius Black had betrayed his parents, he feels hatred coursing through him. (PA, Ch. 11)

Covertly - Secretly, as not to be observed. Harry covertly watches how Umbridge behaves as she inspects Prof. Trelawney's classroom. (OP, Ch. 15)

Cowering - Shrinking from something one finds horrible or frightening. Harry finds Mrs. Weasley cowering from a boggart that has transformed itself into an image of Ron's dead body. (OP, Ch. 9) Harry sees the Dursleys cowering as floating wine glasses rap on their heads. (HBP, Ch. 3)

Cravat - Necktie. Before attending Aragog's funeral, Slughorn decides his tie might be a bit too *exuberant* for the occasion and changes into a *somber* black cravat. (HBP, Ch. 22)

Creditable - Believable. When Umbridge orders Harry to write lines, he asks, in a creditable tone, what to write. (OP, Ch 13)

Crescendo - A gradual rise to a loud sound or powerful feeling. Before fighting his dragon in the Triwizard competition, Harry's feelings of panic rise into a crescendo. (GF, Ch. 20)

Crestfallen - Overwhelmed with disappointment. Hagrid is crestfallen when students complain they had no idea how to open the Monster Book of Monsters. (PA, Ch. 6) Harry can imagine Hagrid's crestfallen and *disbelieving* face if he fails in his task in the Triwizard competition. (GF, Ch. 26)

Crimson - Red. Fawkes, Prof. Dumbledore's phoenix, is crimson. (CS, Ch. 17) Looking up from his hospital bed, Harry sees a sky streaked with *indigo* and crimson and realizes the Quidditch match is over. (HBP, Ch. 19)

Cringing - Bending over in a frightened way. Sirius Black calls Peter Pettigrew a "cringing piece of filth." (PA, Ch. 18)

Crinolines - A stiff skirt, sometimes called a hoop skirt. Women wear crinolines in one of the paintings in Hogwarts castle. (PA, Ch. 6)

Croakily - In a hoarse voice. Frank Bryce, a devoted employee of the Riddle family, yelled croakily at boys who trespassed on Riddle property. (GF, Ch. 1)

Crone - An old, ugly witch. Harry gets to Hogsmeade through an entrance inside the hump of the statue of the one-eyed witch, whom Fred calls a crone. (PA, Ch. 10)

Cronies - An insulting term for the loyal friends of a unworthy leader. Crabbe and Goyle are Malfoy's cronies. (GF, Ch. 10)

Crude - Rough, unsophisticated or rude. When Dumbledore figures out that the way to gain entrance to a seaside hiding place for a Horcrux is to use blood, he says, "So crude." (HBP, Ch. 26)

Cuffs - Hits with the palm of one's hand. Hagrid is so pleased with Harry and Ron for their roles in defeating Voldemort and rescuing Ginny at the end of Book II that he cuffs them on the shoulders, and they fall into their plates of *trifle*. (CS, Ch. 18)

Culminated - Came to a high point or key moment. Tension between Gryffindor and Slytherin before a Quidditch match led to scuffles and culminated in an incident in which two students were treated in the hospital wing for leeks sprouting out of their ears. (PA, Ch. 15) Leanne argues with Katie Bell about the *advisability* of transporting strange objects, which culminated in a tussle on their way to Hogwarts. (HBP, Ch. 12)

Culprit - Evildoer, crook. Prof. McGonagall says that once those who have been petrified can be cured with ripe mandrakes, she is hopeful their information will lead to capturing the culprit who attacked them. (CS, Ch. 16)

Cultivated - Grown. In his fifth year, Ron consults a brochure about careers in the cultivated fungus trade. (OP, Ch. 29)

Cunning - Cleverness. Dumbledore asks if Harry has used all of his cunning to *extract* and important memory from Slughorn. (HBP, Ch. 20)

Cunningly - Cleverly. Karkaroff relates that Mad-Eye Moody once destroyed a carriage clock that was sent to him as a gift because he convinced himself that it was a cunningly disguised basilisk egg. (GF, Ch. 17)

Cur - Dog. Sir Cadogan, on duty in the portrait hole, calls Harry a *"mangy* cur." (PA, Ch. 9)

Curtly - Speaking in a quick and almost rude way. Harry overhears Uncle Vernon speaking curtly to someone delivering a letter from Mrs. Weasley. (GF, Ch. 3) Snape announces curtly that he will go to bed. (GF, Ch. 25) After escaping from Malfoy's attack on the Hogwarts Express, Harry curtly tells his friends he will describe what happened later. (HBP, Ch.7)

Dank - Unpleasantly moist. Outside the Shrieking Shack is a dank, overgrown garden. (PA, Ch. 14)

Darning - Sewing to fix a hole. Harry sees Charlie darning a fireproof *balaclava* that he no doubt uses while working with dragons. (GF, Ch. 10)

Daubed - Smeared. The mystery of who daubed threatening messages on Hogwart's walls is explained in *Harry Potter and the Chamber of Secrets*. (CS, Ch. 17)

Dawning - Spreading slowly but completely, like light at dawn. Snape's face shows an expression of *dawning* comprehension when he sees the Marauder's Map lying on the staircase, near an egg belonging to a Triwizard champion. (GF, Ch. 25)

Deciphered - Figured out, especially something hard to understand immediately. The future may be deciphered by stargazing, Prof. Trelawney says. (GF, Ch. 13)

Decisive - Able to make decisions quickly and firmly. Dumbledore says he thinks Rufus Scrimgeour is a more decisive person than Cornelius Fudge. (HBP, Ch. 4)

Decontaminating - Cleaning out harmful material. When Harry arrives at 12 Grimmauld Place, Hermione tells him they are busy decontaminating the place. (OP, Ch. 4)

Decrepit - Old, worn-out. When Harry first sees Fawkes, the phoenix, the bird is decrepit-looking. (CS, Ch. 12)

Deduce - Figure out by logic. Dumbledore says it's not hard to deduce how Merope came to be abandoned by Tom Riddle, Sr. (HBP, Ch. 10)

Deferentially - With respect and a willingness to bend to another's wishes. Harry notices that Umbridge speaks deferentially to Madam Marchbanks, a Ministry of March official who administers OWL exams. (OP, Ch. 31)

Defiance - Bold challenge. Harry delivers a flask of a potion he brewed to Prof. Snape with mingled feelings of defiance and relief. (OP, Ch. 15)

Defiantly - Boldly challenging authority or power. When Voldemort calls Frank Bryce a Muggle, he says defiantly, "What's that you're calling me?" (GF, Ch. 1) After Winky disapproves of how Dobby talks about the Malfoys, he says defiantly, "They isn't my masters anymore, Winky!" (GF, Ch. 21) Harry tries to anger Ron as a way of *provoking* him to adopt a defiant, goal-saving attitude, but this *strategy* doesn't work. (HBP, Ch. 14)

Deficient - Not up to the task. The Prime Minister thinks that although he's obviously deficient when it comes to materializing in fireplaces, he might have a better grip on governmental responsibilities than Cornelius Fudge does on his. (HBP, Ch. 1)

Deflate - Grow smaller, like a balloon losing air. After Mrs. Weasley notices that Mr. Weasley has used Muggle medicine — stitches — he seems to deflate under her gaze. (OP, Ch. 23)

Deformed - Misshapen. Harry thinks blast-ended screwts looked like deformed, shell-less lobsters. (GF, Ch. 13)

Dejectly - Sadly. Wood speaks dejectly about not winning the Quidditch cup for two years in a row. (PA, Ch. 8)

Dilapidated - Worn, run-down. Prof. Lupin has a dilapidated suitcase. (PA, Ch. 5)

Delegate - To ask someone lower in rank to perform a task. When Harry asks Snape why he was chosen to deliver Occlumency lessons, Snape says he supposes it's because it is the headmaster's privilege to delegate less pleasant tasks. (OP, Ch. 24)

Delegation - Group representing a school or nation. Beaubatons and Durmstrang sent delegations to Hogwarts that stayed for most of the academic year. (GF, Ch. 12)

Deliberated - Thought though. Harry deliberated whether to answer honestly Rufus Scrimgeour's question about Dumbledore's discussions with him about the prophecy. (HBP, Ch. 16)

Deliberately - On purpose. Umbridge accuses Snape of being deliberately unhelpful in her efforts to get the truth out of Harry. (OP, Ch. 32)

Deluded - In the condition of believing something that is not true. Dumbledore says Death Eaters who believe that they are close to Voldemort are deluded, because no one can be close to him. (HBP, Ch. 13)

Delusional - Operating under a false view of reality. *The Daily Prophet* says Mad-Eye Moody is delusional. (OP, Ch. 15)

Demeanor - Behavior toward others. Umbridge has a fussy, *simpering* demeanor. (OP, Ch. 29)

Demise - Death. Rita Skeeter describes Harry as "*deprived* of love since the *tragic* demise of his parents." (GF, Ch. 27)

Deplore - Say something is terrible. Dumbledore tells Harry they should go to The Burrow so they don't *deprive* Molly Weasley of the opportunity to deplore Harry's skinny condition. (HBP, Ch. 4)

Depraved - Evil. When Madam Pince sees the markings in Harry's potions text, she calls him depraved and angrily describes the marked-up book as *despoiled, desecrated* and *befouled*. (HBP, Ch. 15)

Deprive - Take away or withhold something of value. Dumbledore tells Harry they should go to The Burrow so they don't deprive Molly Weasley of the opportunity to *deplore* Harry's skinny condition. (HBP, Ch. 4) Rita Skeeter describes Harry as "deprived of love since the *tragic demise* of his parents." (GF, Ch. 27)

Derelict - Abandoned and run-down; can also mean irresponsible. The Riddle house is described as derelict. (GF, Ch. 1)

Derision - Scorn. Harry cannot keep a tone of derision out of his voice when Slughorn makes excuses for wanting to stay in hiding rather than teach at Hogwarts. (HBP, Ch. 4)

Derisive - Scornful. Malfoy gives a derisive laugh about Percy Weasley playing detective. (CS, Ch. 12)

Descended - Went down. Moody was tough but never descended to the level of the Death Eaters, who hurt their enemies even when it was unnecessary. (GF, Ch. 27)

Descent - Ancestry. The Malfoys consider Hermione inferior because she is of Muggle descent. (GF, Ch. 8)

Desecrated - Mistreated. When Madam Pince sees the markings in Harry's potions text, she angrily describes the marked-up book as *despoiled*, desecrated and *befouled*. (HBP, Ch. 15)

Despicable - Disgusting and without honor. Madame Pomfrey says an attack on Prof. McGonagall by Ministry of Magic officials was despicable. (OP, Ch. 32)

Despoiled - Ruined, robbed of value. When Madam Pince sees the markings in Harry's potions text, she angrily describes the marked-up book as despoiled, *desecrated* and *befouled*. (HBP, Ch. 15)

Destabilize - Make less powerful or take out of control. Sirius says its frightening for Fudge to face the fact that Voldemort is back, which is why Fudge has chosen to convince himself that tales of Voldemort's return are just lies that Dumbledore is telling to destabilize him as minister. (OP, Ch. 5) When Dumbledore says that the D.A. was his idea, Fudge views this as a confession of an effort to destabilize him as minister. (OP, Ch. 27)

Desultory - Done in a random way, without an organization or strategy. After an exam, Harry and Ron sit in the warm air and play a desultory game of wizard chess. (OP, Ch. 31)

Detrimental - Having a negative effect. Dumbledore thinks that Voldemort created multiple Horcruxes so that if one was destroyed, it would not be so detrimental as to be a form of death. (HBP, Ch. 23)

Detritus - Debris, loose remains. The Gryffindor common room is usually full of detritus such as wadded-up bits of parchment, old Gobstones and candy wrappers. (OP, Ch. 14)

Devious - Intent on deceiving others for personal gain. Rita Skeeter writes that Viktor Krum is *smitten* with the "devious" Hermione Granger. (GF, Ch. 27)

Devoid - Empty. After being hit with stupefying spells, the Hungarian Horntail nostrils were devoid of flame. (GF, Ch. 19)

Devoutly - Seriously and sincerely. Harry is devoutly thankful that Ron cannot perform Legilimency because Harry thinks about Ginny a lot. (HBP, Ch. 15)

Dewy - Innocent. After Hermione stalks out of Divination, Lavender Brown reminds Prof. Trelawney that she predicted they would lose one of their number around Easter, and Prof. Trelawney smiles a dewy smile. (PA, Ch. 15)

Diatribe - Long, emotional speech, usually to criticize something. In a silent lunch, Harry could tell that Aunt Petunia had *suppressed* a diatribe complaining about the strange ways of the wizarding world. (GF, Ch. 4)

Dictates - Commands, requires. Dumbledore says that courtesy dictates that one not apparate into a wizard's home but knock on the door. (HBP, Ch. 4)

Dilapidated - Worn out. The armchairs in the Gryffindor common room are dilapidated. (OP, Ch. 11) Narcissa Malfoy discovers that Severus Snape lives in a dilapidated brick house. (HBP, Ch. 2)

Diluting - The process of making a liquid or color weaker. Before using the Portkey, Harry sees the first rays of sunlight diluting the "inky blackness" of the night sky. (GF, Ch. 6)

Diminished - Lessened, reduced. Dumbledore says that without his Horcruxes, Voldemort will be "a *mortal* man with a *maimed* and diminished soul." (HBP, Ch. 23)

Din - The noise of a crowded room. After Snape insulted Hermione about the size of her front teeth, Ron and Harry shouted at him but he could not hear the names they were calling him because of the din in the corridor. (GF, Ch. 18)

Dire - Desperate. Hermione gives Harry dire warnings that he will be making a mistake if he breaks into Umbridge's office. (OP, Ch. 29)

Disabuse - Explain something isn't true. After Hagrid says the Malfoys wouldn't dare make trouble on Diagon Alley, Harry and Hermione want to disabuse him of that notion. (HBP, Ch. 6)

Disarray - Messiness. After he became a Triwizard champion, Harry felt like his mind was in complete disarray. (GF, Ch. 17)

Disbanded - Stopped functioning as a group. The Death Eaters disbanded after Voldemort disappeared. (GF, Ch. 2)

Disbelief - State of doubting. Disbelief is *etched* all over Fudge's face when Hermione tells him she heard an *incantation* spoken before the Dark Mark appeared. (GF, Ch. 9)

Disbelieving - Shocked, finding it hard to accept a truth. Harry can imagine Hagrid's *crestfallen* and *disbelieving* face if he fails in his task in the Triwizard competition. (GF, Ch. 26)

Discarded - Got rid of. Harry kept checking Ron's watch because he had discarded his own. (GF, Ch. 29)

Discomfited - In a state of feeling unsure and uneasy. Bellatrix LeStrange looks discomfited when Snape suggests that the only way he could be disloyal to the Dark Lord would be if he had *hoodwinked* him, which he suggests is impossible. (HBP, Ch. 2)

Discomforted - In a state of feeling annoyed and uneasy. Amos Diggory looks discomforted when he is criticized by Barty Crouch for accusing Harry of conjuring the Dark Mark. (GF, Ch. 9)

Discomposed - Upset enough to appear to lose one's composure. When conferring with Snape in the garden, Karkaroff appears discomposed when he catches sight of Ron and Harry nearby. (GF, Ch. 23)

Disconcerting - Disturbing. At age 11, Harry found it disconcerting that everyone in the wizarding world knew his name. (GF, Ch. 2)

Disconsolate - Unhappy. In Mr. Weasley's office at the Ministry of Magic, Harry sees a enchanted toaster hiccupping in a disconsolate way. (OP, Ch. 7)

Disconsolately - Sadly. George looks disconsolately at the night sky before a Quidditch match with Hufflepuff. (OP, Ch. 26)

Discord - Conflict, disagreement. The Sorting Hat sings in year five that at first there was little *strife* among Hogwarts' founders, but then discord crept in. (OP, Ch. 11)

Discredit - Injure the reputation of a person. Fudge tries to discredit Dumbledore by removing him from some of the more prestigious wizarding councils; according to Bill Weasley, Dumbledore said he doesn't care as long as they don't take his card out of the Chocolate Frogs. (OP, Ch. 5) Dumbledore says Lucius Malfoy slipped Tom Riddle's diary to Ginny Weasley in an effort to discredit Arthur Weasley and get rid of an *incriminating* object at the same time. (HBP, Ch. 23)

Disdainful - Full of dislike. Malfoy pats Buckbeak's head with a disdainful expression. (PA, Ch. 6)

Disembodied - Without a body. Harry hears a disembodied voice at Hogwarts muttering about killing. (CS, Ch. 14) Dudley's head poking out of his pajamas looks disembodied to Harry. (HBP, Ch. 3)

Disembowelment - Ripping out someone's guts. Filch threatened Fred and George with disembowelment, according to the twins, who were probably exaggerating. (PA, Ch. 10)

Disentangled - Unknotted. Landing in a jumble after using the Portkey, Harry got up and disentangled himself from Ron. (GF, Ch. 7) After disentangling himself from a hedgerow into which he had fallen, Harry urges Hagrid to help Katie Bell, who was behaving strangely after a visit to Hogsmeade. (HBP, Ch. 12)

Disfigures - Makes ugly. Before Harry can answer Rita Skeeter's first question, her Quick-Quotes Quill writes, "An ugly scar, souvenir of a tragic past, disfigures the otherwise charming face of Harry Potter." (GF, Ch. 18)

Disgorging - Spitting out. The Prime Minister sees emerald green flames in his fireplace, followed by the disgorging of a wizard on to the rug. (HBP, Ch. 1)

Disgruntled - In a bad mood because of something that just happened. Hermione is disgruntled when Defense Against the Dark Arts is canceled. (CS, Ch.. 18)

Disheveled - Messy. Harry observes that Lucius Malfoy's usually *sleek* hair was disheveled. (CS, Ch. 18) Upon waking, Harry sees two disheveled figures, whom he soon realizes are Fred and George. (GF, Ch. 6) After several visits from Cornelius Fudge, the Prime Minister is quite disturbed to see him emerge from the fireplace once again, looking more disheveled and *fretful* than ever. (HBP, Ch. 1)

Dismal - Awful, sad. The *atmosphere* is dismal in the Gryffindor common room after a Quidditch loss to Hufflepuff. (OP, Ch. 26)

Dismally - Dreadfully. Lupin says he was appointed prefect with the hope that he would exert some control over his mischievous friends, but that he failed dismally. (OP, Ch. 9)

Dismissively - In a superior and unconcerned way. Fleur Delacour speaks dismissively about Hogwarts' decorations, saying those at Beaubatons are much more impressive. (GF, Ch. 23) When students say they want to learn how to use defensive spells, Umbridge treats their concerns dismissively. (OP, Ch. 12) When Hermione gives an excellent answer in class, Snape dismissively suggests she was just reciting an entry from a book. (HBP, Ch. 9)

Disorientated - Confused, losing one's sense of time or place. Mr. Weasley says that if a person's memory is modified, they might be disorientated for a while. (GF, Ch. 10)

Disoriented - Same as disorientated. Harry felt disoriented after seeing Ginny kiss Dean Thomas. (HBP, Ch. 14)

Disparagingly - In a way to make a person feel small or without value. When Luna says her father is an editor who doesn't think much of *The Daily Prophet*, Rita Skeeter looks at her disparagingly and suggests that her father can't be anyone important. (OP, Ch. 25)

Disparate - Different and unrelated. Slughorn that making an antidote for a combination of disparate poisons requires something in addition to a specific antidote for each poison in the mixture. (HBP, Ch. 18)

Dispassionately - Without emotion. When Harry makes a negative comment about Hermione's decision to bring Cormac McLaggen to a party as a date, Hermione says dispassionately that she hoped to annoy Ron. (HBP, Ch. 15)

Dispiritedly - Sadly, without enthusiasm. Harry wanders dispiritedly toward the library when his friends are all in Hogsmeade. (PA, Ch. 8) When his Patronus fails to charge a dementor formed by a boggart, Harry talks dispiritedly about it to Prof. Lupin. (PA, Ch. 11)

Displeasure - Unhappiness, disappointment. Snape says Voldemort's *initial* displeasure with him evaporated once he realized how useful Snape could be to him as a spy. (HBP, Ch. 2)

Disposed - Of a mind to do something. No one seemed disposed to follow Hagrid into the Forbidden Forest. (OP, Ch. 21)

Disrepute - Shame, disgrace. Lucius Malfoy tells *The Daily Prophet* that Arthur Weasley's involvement with an enchanted car has "brought the Ministry into disrepute." (CS, Ch. 12)

Disservice - Bad deed. Dumbledore says Harry would do his friends a disservice if he did not tell them about the prophecy. (HBP, Ch. 4)

Dissuade - Persuade not to do something. Hermione keeps up a stream of *admonitions* to try to dissuade Harry from his plan to break into Umbridge's office in order to use her fireplace to communicate with Sirius. (OP, Ch. 29)

Distinct - Clear. While hidden under his invisibility cloak, Harry gets the distinct impression that Mrs. Norris can smell him. (GF, Ch. 25) Luna Lovegood gives people an impression of distinct *dottiness*. (OP, Ch. 10)

Distinctions - Differences. Snape says Harry is a *lamentable* potions-maker because he lacks the ability to sense fine distinctions. (OP, Ch. 24)

Distinctive - Unique and characteristic of someone. Mad-Eye Moody has a wooden foot that makes a distinctive clunking sound when he walks. (GF, Ch. 14)

Distorted - Twisted out of shape. Harry looks at his distorted reflection in a spoon. (HBP, Ch. 8)

Distractedly - In a manner that suggests someone is not really paying attention because he or she is concerned with something else. A ministry wizard patrolling the grounds of the Quidditch World Cup mutters distractedly when he sees children playing on broomsticks in broad daylight. (GF, Ch. 7)

(In a) Dither - State of being unsettled, excited or confused. When Ron is made a prefect, his mother is in a dither. (OP, Ch. 9)

Dither (verb) - To be unsettled, excited or confused. Madam Malkin dithers after Harry and Draco get into an argument in her shop. (HBP, Ch. 6)

Diversion - A distraction that absorbs one's attention. Neville created a diversion when he ate one of Fred and George's custard creams and turned into a canary. (GF, Ch. 21) Fred brags about his Decoy Detonators, which you drop *surreptitiously* when you want to create a diversion. (HBP, Ch. 6)

Docilely - Cooperatively. Harry notices that Kreacher's bitter mutterings had *subsided*, and that he was taking orders more docilely. (OP, Ch. 24)

Doddery - Old and easily fooled. Hermione says the committee hearing Buckbeak's case is full of "doddery old fools," and that Malfoy's father had influenced them. (PA, Ch. 15)

Dodgy - In England, dishonest or unreliable. Hagrid calls Knockturn Alley a dodgy place. (CS, Ch. 4) Ron says he thinks the plan to use Polyjuice Potion sounds "a bit dodgy... What if we were stuck looking like three Slytherins forever?" (CS, Ch. 9)

Dolefully - Sadly. Harry and Ron's owls hoot dolefully. (OP, Ch. 6)

Dollops - Lumps. Hermione serves the jelly-like Polyjuice Potion by putting dollops of it in three glasses. (CS, Ch. 12)

Domains - Areas of control. Igor Karkaroff asks Dumbledore, "We are all protective of our private domains, are we not?" (GF, Ch. 23)

Doom - Death or unhappy ending. Ron, suspecting the Polyjuice Potion plan will go wrong, looks at Harry with a "doom-*laden* expression." (CS, Ch. 12)

Dottiness - State of being a little crazy, usually in an amusing way. Luna Lovegood wears a necklace of butterbeer caps, creating an impression of *distinct* dottiness. (OP, Ch. 10)

Doused - Suddenly hit with a large amount of liquid. When Snape tells Narcissa Malfoy that she should keep Voldemort's secrets, she "gasped as though he had doused her with cold water." (HBP, Ch. 2)

Downright - Absolutely. Uncle Vernon looked downright alarmed when Harry informed him that the Weasleys would be arriving on Privet Drive the next day. (GF, Ch. 4)

Dramatically - With great emphasis, as if making a speech in a play. When Harry tells Slughorn that he cannot attend another of his parties, Slughorn says dramatically, "Unlucky again!" (HBP, Ch. 12)

Draught ("draft") - Drink. In a Herbology text, Harry reads about plants used in "Confusing and Befuddlement Draughts." (OP, Ch. 18)

Drawling - A slow form of speech in which vowel sounds are drawn out. Draco Malfoy speaks in a bored, drawling voice. (SS, Ch. 5)

Drawn - With a tired face. Harry notices that Tonks looks drawn. (HBP, Ch. 5)

Dreading - Hating an upcoming event. Prof. Trelawney advises Lavender Brown, "That thing you are dreading — it will happen on Friday the sixteenth of October." (PA, Ch. 6)

Dregs - Solid clumps of soggy material left after a liquid is drained from a container. Prof. Trelawney asks students to drink tea (made with tea leaves, not tea bags) until only dregs are left in the cup, then to look for shapes in the dregs. (PA, Ch. 6) Before a Quidditch match, a depressed Ron peered into the dregs of his cereal as if he was "seriously considering attempting to drown himself in them." (OP, Ch. 19)

Drone - A dull speaking voice that goes on and on. Prof. Binns lectures in a *monotonous* drone. (OP, Ch. 17)

Droned - Spoke on and on. Harry sank in to *stupor* as Oliver Wood droned on about Quidditch *tactics*. (CS, Ch. 7)

Dubious — Doubtful; prompting suspicion. Wizards trying to start fires using matches have dubious looks on their faces, as if they are sure this couldn't possibly work. (GF, Ch. 7) Harry realizes that the Marauder's Map is a dubious magical object. (GF, Ch. 25)

Dulcet - Sweet-sounding. George beams at Harry, saying, "We thought we heard your dulcet tones." (OP, Ch. 4)

Dumbfounded - Puzzled. Pansy Parkinson looks dumbfounded when Malfoy hints that he will be working for Voldemort soon. (HBP, Ch. 7)

Dumbstruck - Stunned into silence. Ron is dumbstruck when Harry states his scar has been hurting him. (GF, Ch. 10) Hogwarts students and teachers are dumbstruck after Dumbledore is killed. (HBP, Ch. 27)

Dunghill - Pile of manure; something repulsive. Narcissa Malfoy finds Severus Snape's home in a *labyrinth* of *dilapidated* buildings in an area that Bellatrix LeStrange calls a "Muggle dunghill." (HBP, Ch. 2)

Dustbins - In England, trash cans. Mad-Eye Moody got a reputation for being too quick to use his wand when he attacked his own dustbins. (GF, Ch. 14)

Earnestly - With strong belief. Hermione speaks earnestly when she says she wants to take Muggle Studies to understand Muggles from the wizarding point of view. (PA, Ch. 4) Ludo Bagman earnestly says that he had no idea Rookwood was allied with Voldemort before he passed information to him, but is sentenced to Azkaban nevertheless. (GF, Ch. 30)

Ebbing - Dwindling. Harry felt his anger ebbing away. (OP, Ch. 2)

Eccentric - Odd in thought or behavior, suggesting a touch of madness. *The Daily Prophet* says Dumbledore is known for "eccentric decisions" including "the hiring of werewolf Remus Lupin, half-giant Rubeus Hagrid and *delusional* ex-auror 'Mad-Eye' Moody." (OP, Ch. 15) When Dumbledore wears a plum-colored, velvet suit to an orphanage that houses Tom Riddle, a girl who opens the door is stunned by his eccentric appearance. (HBP, Ch. 11)

Ecstasy - Enormous pleasure. In a kind of "miserable ecstasy," Dobby moans about how wonderful Harry is. (CS, Ch. 10)

Ecstatic - Incredibly happy. Ron is ecstatic when he gets a new broomstick. (OP, Ch. 9) Harry senses that Voldemort is ecstatic and later reads the news that 10 Death Eaters have escaped from Azkaban. (OP, Ch. 24)

Efficacious - Effective. In a Herbology text, Harry reads about plants that are efficacious in inflaming the brain and are used in "Confusing and Befuddlement *Draughts*." (OP, Ch. 18) Slughorn says that most authorities agree that it is most efficacious to pick certain plants at twilight. (HBP, Ch. 22)

Ejecting - Throwing out or spitting out. Harry and Dumbledore hear *raucous* shouting outside the Three Broomsticks as they see Madame Rosmerta ejecting a wizard. (HBP, Ch. 25)

Elaborate (verb, pronounced "ee-LAB-or-ate") - Expand upon. Harry hoped Dumbledore would elaborate on the subject of his private lessons, but the headmaster did not. (HBP, Ch. 4)

Elation - Great happiness. Harry's feeling of elation after drinking Felix Felicis increases after he hears Ginny and Dean Thomas get into a quarrel, which Harry realizes might end up making Ginny available to date him. (HBP, Ch. 22)

Elephantine - Huge. The Beaubaton's carriage is pulled by elephantine horses that drink only single-malt whiskey. (GF, Ch. 16)

Elite - The upper few. Aurors are an elite in the wizarding world. (OP, Ch. 12)

Elixir - Liquid with medical or magical properties. Ron promised to *reimburse* Harry for an elixir to improve his ability to think during exams, but Hermione *confiscated* it. (OP, Ch. 31)

Elongated - Stretched out. Harry's feet become elongated, like flippers, after he chews gillyweed. (GF, Ch. 4)

Eloping - Getting married in secret. Molly Weasley says that when Voldemort first came to power, it prompted lots of nervous reactions, which included people eloping. (HBP, Ch. 5)

Eloquent - Highly expressive. When Narcissa Malfoy asks Snape for help, her desperation shows on her face, which is eloquent with despair. (HBP, Ch. 2)

Eluding - Escaping notice or capture. Sirius Black is described by *The Daily Prophet* as "still eluding capture." (PA, Ch. 3)

Elusive - Hard to locate or obtain. The snitch is elusive. (HBP, Ch. 14)

Emanate - Give off. Fleur Delacour's hair seems to emanate a silvery glow. (HBP, Ch. 5)

Embargo - A government's ban on certain goods being bought or sold by people in different countries. Mr. Weasley stands behind the ministry's embargo on flying carpets. (GF, Ch. 7)

Embarked - Began. Prof. McGonagall's class had embarked on the *immensely* difficult topic of human Transfiguration. (HBP, Ch. 15)

Emblazoned - Decorated with an image or words. The Monster Book of Monsters is emblazoned with a golden letters. (PA, Ch. 1) A purple *leaflet* in Harry's trunk is emblazoned with the words "Ministry of Magic" and gives safety instructions. (HBP, Ch. 3)

Emboldened - Made brave. Emboldened by Harry's success in approaching Buckbeak, other Hogwarts students approached Hippogriffs. (PA, Ch. 6)

Embossed - Decorated with. Mundungus Fletcher shows a lot of interest in a silver goblet at 12 Grimmauld Place, which Sirius describes as fine goblin-made silver, embossed with the Black family crest. Mundungus mutters that the crest could be removed. (OP, Ch. 5)

Embraced - Hugged or accepted. Snape says that after he told Dumbledore how much her regretted his time as a Death Eater, the headmaster embraced him with open arms. (HBP, Ch. 2)

Embroidered - Sewed with decorative patterns. Dumbledore wore a magnificent green robe embroidered with many stars and moons. (GF, Ch. 12)

Embroidering - Adding to a story. The *inhabitants* of Little Hangleton tell tales of what happened in the Riddle house, often embroidering the tale. (GF, Ch. 1)

Emerged - Came out. After the Quidditch World Cup, Ludo Bagman emerged from some trees, and Harry noticed that he no longer looked *buoyant* and rosy-faced. (GF, Ch. 9)

Emitting - Issuing forth. Before the Dark Mark appears, Harry sees flashes of light emitting from something moving across the Quidditch Field. (GF, Ch. 9)

Emphatically - Forcefully. When people ask Harry if he thinks Mr. Weasley has been injured, he emphatically says yes. (OP, Ch. 22)

Encased - Enclosed in a solid material. Wormtail's hand is encased in bright silver glove. (HBP, Ch. 2)

Enclosure - Fenced-in area. Harry battles a Hungarian Horntail in an enclosure. (GF, Ch. 20)

Encompassed - Included. Cornelius Fudge explains to the Prime Minister that the responsibilities of the Ministry of Magic encompassed everything from broomstick regulations to keeping the dragon population under control. (HBP, Ch. 1)

Encounter - Meeting. Harry's memory of his last face-to-face encounter with Dumbledore is not a pleasant one, because Harry behaved so badly. (HBP, Ch. 4)

Encrusted - Penetrated with or decorated with. The goblet of fire is encrusted with jewels. (GF, Ch. 16)

Encumbered - Weighed down by something. Dumbledore says he and Harry don't want to be encumbered by luggage, so he uses magic to send Harry's trunk to The Burrow. (HBP, Ch. 3)

Endear - Make beloved. Harry's sloppy appearance did not endear him to the neighbors on Privet Drive. (OP, Ch. 1)

Endurance - State of enduring. When apparating with Dumbledore, Harry feels as if he is being compressed beyond endurance. (HBP, Ch. 25)

Endure - Put up with. After Rita Skeeter prints lies about Harry in *The Daily Prophet*, he has to endure people quoting the article to him. (GF, Ch. 19) Bellatrix LeStrange tells Snape that she endured the dementors in Azkaban while he was comfortably living at Hogwarts. (HBP, Ch. 2)

Engenders - Brings with it. "Envy engenders spite," Voldemort tells Dumbledore. (HBP, Ch. 20)

Engraved - Cut into stone. At Grigotts Bank a poem that warns against theft is engraved in a set of doors. (SS, Ch. 6)

Engrossed - Fully involved in. Witches and wizards in portraits are sometimes engrossed in their own conversations. (OP, Ch. 12)

Enigmatic - Puzzling. Dumbledore ends one of his first in-depth conversations with Harry about Lord Voldemort on an enigmatic note. (HBP, Ch. 13)

Enmity - Hatred. Voldemort's gift for spreading *discord* and enmity is great. (OP, Ch. 12) After a Quidditch victory, Ron is in a good mood, all enmity forgotten. (HBP, Ch. 14)

Enraptured - Totally absorbed or in love. Hagrid gazed, enraptured, at the dragons the Charlie Weasley brought to the Triwizard Tournament. (GF, Ch. 19)

Ensconced - Concealed or settled. Once Harry and his friends were safely ensconced at the Gryffindor table, he told them about the instructions he found written in his Potions textbook. (HBP, Ch 9)

Enslaving - Making prisoner. Dumbledore guesses that Merope could not bear to continue her relationship with Tom Riddle by enslaving him with magic. (HBP, Ch. 10)

Ensure - Make sure. Mr. Ollivander inspects the Triwizard Champions' wands before the tournament to ensure they are in good working condition. (GF, Ch. 18) Rita Skeeter writes that Dumbledore has a duty to ensure that Harry Potter and other Hogwarts students are warned about the dangers of associating with part-giants. (GF, Ch. 24) Voldemort tells Harry that a faithful Death Eater put Harry's name in the Goblet of Fire to ensure that Harry would be in the tournament. (GF, Ch. 33) By delaying responding to Voldemort's call until Dumbledore told him to go, Snape ensured that Dumbledore would continue to trust him. (HBP, Ch. 2) Slughorn turns his body near the fire to ensure an even heat on his backside. (HBP, Ch. 4)

Entwined - Twisted together. In the Chamber of Secrets, Harry follows a windy tunnels until he reaches a wall decorated with a carving of entwined serpents. (CS, Ch. 16) Harry sees Ron and Lavender Brown entwined in the same armchair. (HBP, Ch. 15)

Enumerate - List. Students hear Prof. Grubbly-Plank is enumerating the magical properties of unicorns. (GF, Ch 24) The Prime Minister is troubled that his political opponent had gone on television to enumerate all the awful things that had happened during the prior week and why they were all the government's fault. (HBP, Ch.1)

Enviously - Jealously. After Prof. McGonagall gives Harry a Nimbus 2000, Ron enviously says that he's never even touched one. (SS, Ch. 7)

Envisaged - Imagined. Dumbledore says Voldemort probably envisaged Hogwarts as good place to recruit young wizards. (HBP, Ch. 20)

Envoys - People sent to establish communications between nations or tribes who have not been talking. Dumbledore proposes sending envoys to the Giants in anticipation of a war with dark Wizards. (GF, Ch. 36)

Erected - Built. At Quality Quidditch Supplies, Harry sees the Firebolt sitting on a newly erected platform. (PA, Ch. 4)

Erectly - Straight up. Hermione walks erectly toward the door before turning and cursing Ron. (HBP, Ch. 14)

Eruption - An outburst. There was an eruption of cheers from the Slytherin end of the Quidditch field when Slytherin scored. (PA, Ch. 15)

Escort - Go with as a companion. After Prof. Lockhart removes bones from Harry's arms instead of repairing them, he suggests Ron and Hermione escort Harry to the hospital wing. (CS, Ch. 10) Dumbledore writes Harry a note offering to escort him from Privet Drive to the Burrow. (HBP, Ch. 3) Mrs. Weasley seems *flustered* with the *austere* manner of Aurors escorting Harry and her children to Kings Cross Station. (HBP, Ch. 7)

Estrangement - State of isolation from others. Percy's disagreements with his family lead to his estrangement. (OP, Ch. 9)

Etched - Dug into. Disbelief is etched all over Fudge's face when Hermione tells him she heard an *incantation* spoken before the Dark Mark appeared. (GF, Ch. 9)

Euphoria - Feeling fantastic. Harry felt euphoria after Gryffindor defeated Slytherin in Quidditch, and it lasted a week. (PA, Ch. 16)

Evasively - As to avoid a subject. Cornelius Fudge speaks evasively about what he knows about Sirius Black's intentions. (PA, Ch. 10)

Evidently - Apparently. Mrs. Weasley evidently had waited in the front yard for her family and Harry to return after the Quidditch World Cup. (GF, Ch. 10)

Evoked - Called. Dumbledore says the magic he evoked when Harry was a baby protects Harry as long as he lives at least part of the year on Privet Drive, until the age of 17. (HBP, Ch. 3)

Exacerbated - Worsened. Hufflepuff students' resentment of Harry for throwing into question Cedric's status as Hogwarts champion in the

Triwizard Tournament was worsened by they fact that Hufflepuff hardly ever received any glory. (GF, Ch. 18)

Exasperated - Annoyed, frustrated, fed up. Harry is exasperated with Aunt Petunia when she frets about whether Dudley still has his soul after being attacked by a dementor. (OP, Ch. 2) After Harry finished second in the one of the tasks in Triwizard competition because he decided to save two people, Ron and Hermione gave him "half-exasperated, half-*commiserating* looks." (GF, Ch. 26)

Exasperation - State of being annoyed or frustrated. Ron's face shows mingled surprise and exasperation when Harry orders Dobby and Kreacher to follow Draco. (HBP, Ch. 19)

Excess - Extra amount, too much. Chapter Five of *Harry Potter and the Half-Blood Prince* is called "An Excess of *Phlegm*." (HBP, CH. 5)

Exclusively - Uniquely; in journalism, an exclusive is a bit of news that no other news source has. Rita Skeeter tells her readers that she can exclusively reveal that Hagrid is the son of the giantess Fridwulfa. (GF, Ch. 24)

Excruciating - Extreme, causing pain or anguish. Frustrated in his attempt to see Dumbledore, Harry kicked the gargoyle that guards his office and experienced excruciating pain. (GF, Ch. 29)

Excursion - Trip. Harry learned the Levicorpus spell on an unauthorized excursion into Snape's pensieve. (HBP, Ch. 12)

Executioner - Person hired by the government to carry out a death sentence. Hermione is disturbed that the Ministry of Magic sends an executioner to Hogwarts, because it looks like "they've already decided" Buckbeak's fate even before the hippogriff's *appeal* is heard by the Committee for the Disposal of Dangerous Creatures. (PA, Ch. 16)

Exemplified - Stood as an example. Dumbledore says at Cedric's funeral that he exemplified many of the qualities that distinguish Hufflepuff. (Gf, Ch, 37)

Exempted - Excused from. The Triwizard champions were exempted from end-of-year exams. (GF, Ch. 17)

Exerted - Tried. Dumbledore skeptically asks Harry if he thinks he has exerted his very best effort in trying to get Slughorn's memory of his conversation about Horcruxes with Riddle. (HBP, Ch. 20)

Exhilarating - Tremendously exciting and uplifting. After drinking Felix Felicis, Harry feels an "an exhilarating sense of *infinite* opportunity." (HBP, Ch. 22)

Expectant - Expecting something to occur. Having traveled to the past contained within Riddle's diary, Harry felt tense and expectant, waiting for something revealing to happen. (CS, Ch. 13) Harry's open trunk looks expectant before Dumbledore arrives to take him to Hogwarts. (HBP, Ch. 3)

Explicable - Able to be explained. Dumbledore says that Voldemort's strange, less-than-human appearance was explicable if one imagined that he had performed unusually evil forms of magic. (HBP, Ch. 23)

Explicit - Clearly stated. Harry thinks the hint that Cedric had given him about opening his egg would have been more explicit if Cedric had really intended to be helpful. (GF, Ch. 24)

Expressionless - Without emotion. Tom Riddle speaks in an expressionless voice when admitting he had kept stolen objects in his closet. (HBP, Ch. 13)

Expulsion - The process of being expelled (forced to leave a place). Harry fears expulsion from Hogwarts if he is caught performing magic at Privet Drive while he is underage. (PA, Ch. 2).

Extensive - Big, wide-ranging. Dumbledore said he arranged for Harry to be raised by Muggles because Voldemort's knowledge of magic was so extensive that no spell would have protected Harry in the wizarding world. (OP, Ch. 37)

Extent - Range, scope. Voldemort warns Wormtail to be obedient or face the full extent of Lord Voldemort's *wrath*.

Extinction - Dying out of a group or species. Giants fought among themselves and left so few of their number alive that the race of giants was brought to the point of extinction, Rita Skeeter reports in an article in *The Daily Prophet*. (GF, Ch. 24)

Extract - Take out. Snapes says that though Legilimency, Voldemort is able to extract information from a person's mind such as his feelings and memories. (OP, Ch. 24) Harry thinks about the memory he needs to extract from Slughorn (HBP, Ch. 19)

Extracting - Taking out. Harry sees Dumbledore extracting memories from his mind with his wand and placing them in the pensieve. (GF, Ch. 30)

Extravagant - Big, elaborate or expensive. At the Quidditch World Cup, Harry is shocked at how extravagant some of tents are; among them is a tent with three floors and turrets. (GF, Ch. 7) When Prof. McGonagall says, "That was excellent," Harry considers it extravagant praise, coming from her. (GF, Ch. 20)

Extricated - Removed from a small, confining space. In the Ministry of Magic, Harry sees a wizard carry a load of broomsticks into an elevator; later he extricated himself with difficulty. (OP, Ch. 7)

Exuberant - Gushing with joy. The night before a Quidditch match with Slytherin, Fred and George dealt with the pressure by being more exuberant than ever. (PA, Ch. 15) Dean Thomas is exuberant after a Quidditch win over Hufflepuff. (HBP, Ch. 14) Before attending Aragog's funeral, Slughorn decides his tie might be a bit too exuberant (colorful, joyous) for the occasion and changes into a *somber* black *cravat*. (HBP, Ch. 22)

Exultant - Happy and triumphant. Umbridge looks exultant when Hermione tells her that she knows where Dumbledore has stored a weapon. (OP, Ch. 32) Voldemort looks *rapt* and exultant when his body is restored. (GF, Ch. 33)

Fabled - Famous, legendary. *The Daily Prophet* says a disturbance in the fabled Hall of Prophecy was connected with speculation that Voldemort had returned. (HBP, Ch. 3)

Fair - Having light skin color or blonde hair. Narcissa Malfoy is described as fair while her sister Bellatrix's complexion and hair are dark. (HBP, Ch. 2)

Fathom - Figure. Harry didn't have time to fathom how Hermione was able to take so many classes at the same time. (PA, Ch. 11)

Fathomless - Incapable of being measured or understood. Snapes eyes are fathomless. (GF, Ch. 27)

Fawning - Treating someone like a celebrity. Ron says he bets Viktor Krum is used to people fawning over him. (GF, Ch. 16)

Feeble - Weak. As they approach the entrance to the Chamber of Secrets, Gilderoy Lockhart says in a feeble voice, "Boys, what good will it do?" (CS, Ch. 16) Errol the owl is described as elderly and feeble. (GF, Ch. 3)

Feigning - Faking. Ron and Hermione had a habit of feigning deafness whenever Harry talked about his suspicion that Draco Malfoy was a Death Eater. (HBP, Ch. 13)

Feint - Distracting movement, as when a ballplayer pretends to go in one direction then moves the opposite way. While watching the Quidditch World Cup, Harry sees Krum do dive called the Wronski Defensive Feint. (GF, Ch. 8)

Fen - A tract of wet, spongy land. The Sorting Hat sings that Gryffindor grew up in a *moor*, Ravenclaw in a *glen*, Hufflepuff in a valley and Slytherin in a fen. (GF, Ch. 12)

Fermenting - Occurring in a very active process. The idea of Ron being happy with Ginny finding a new boyfriend was fermenting in Harry's brain. (HBP, Ch. 22)

Ferreting - Sniffing about like a ferret. Rita Skeeter is ferreting around about the disappearance of Bertha Jorkins, Mr. Weasley reports. (GF, Ch. 10)

Fervently - With strong emotion and belief. While engaged in time travel, Harry tells Hermione fervently, "This is the weirdest thing we have ever done." (PA, Ch. 20)

Festive - Happy, celebratory. Fred says he and George have come to give Harry some "festive cheer," then they reveal the Marauder's Map. (PA, Ch. 10)

Festoons - Decorations. At Christmastime, the Great Hall is decorated with festoons of holly. (SS, Ch. 10)

Fettered - Confined, like a person in handcuffs. Firenze says Sybill Trelawney may have some talent, but that, like all humans, she is *blinkered* and fettered "by the limitations of her kind." (OP, Ch. 27)

Fevered - In a state of high emotion. Tom Riddle is fevered when he explains to Dumbledore the talents he possesses. (HBP, Ch. 13)

Feverishly - In an emotional way. Hermione speaks feverishly about her worries about her exam grades. (HBP, Ch. 5)

Fiasco - Disaster. Harry describes his date with Cho Chang as a complete fiasco. (OP, Ch. 26) Dumbledore describes Harry's Occlumency lessons with Snape as a fiasco. (HBP, Ch. 4)

Fissure - Crack. Following Sirius in dog form, Harry, Ron and Hermione slip through a fissure in a rock and find themselves in a cave. (GF, Ch. 27)

Flagon - A large bottle with a handle and a cover. After the first task of the Triwizard Tournament, there are flagons of pumpkin juice and other goodies in the Gryffindor common room. (GF, Ch. 21)

Flagrant - Obvious and undesirable. Fudge says Harry has a flagrant tendency to break rules. (OP, Ch. 8)

Flap - In England, an argument or worried state. Fudge tells Harry that "you've had us all in a right flap" after he ran away from Privet Drive. (PA, Ch. 3)

Flattered - Complimented. Hermione looks flattered after Ron notes that she had been quite bold by walking out on Prof. Trelawney and then giving Malfoy a well-deserved slap. (PA, Ch. 16)

Flattery - The practice of paying compliments to others. Slughorn compliments Tom Riddle on his careful flattery of people who count. (HBP, Ch. 23)

Fleeting - Disappearing or passing quickly. Bellatrix LeStrange's expression of satisfaction is fleeting. (HBP, Ch. 2) After being told he must address Dumbledore as "Professor" or "Sir," Tom Riddle's expression becomes cross for a fleeting moment. (HBP, Ch. 13)

Flickering - Growing brighter and then dimmer. Frank Bryce is curious about a flickering light he sees in the old Riddle house. (GF, Ch. 1)

Flighty - Unpredictable. In a poetic turn of phrase, Dumbledore compares adventure to an attractive but unpredictable woman: "Let us step out into the night and pursue that flighty *temptress*, adventure." (HBP, Ch. 3)

Flinch - Move suddenly, as to avoid a blow. Lord Voldemort tells Wormtail, "I see you flinch when you look at me." (GF, Ch. 1)

Flippant - Lacking seriousness. After Ron jokes about how unlikely it is that Voldemort is hiding in Flourish and Blotts, he realizes it's a bad idea to make such flippant comments. (HBP, Ch. 6)

Flourish - A fancy, unnecessary mark or motion. Ron labeled his last star on his star chart with a flourish. (PA, Ch. 8) Fred produces the Marauder's Map with a flourish. (PA, Ch. 10) After encountering Slughorn on the way to Hagrid's for Aragog's funeral, Harry takes off his invisibility cloak with a flourish. (HBP, Ch. 22)

Flourishing - Healthy and thriving. Dumbledore compliments Mr. Dursley by saying that his flowers are flourishing. (HBP, Ch. 3)

Flouting - Ignoring, with contempt. After Ron is named prefect, Percy writes to him to say he is glad that Ron has decided to stop flouting authority and shoulder some responsibility. (OP, Ch. 14)

Flummoxed - Baffled. Mr. Weasley says that a wizard has been making Muggle toilets *regurgitate* when flushed, and that Muggle plumbers are flummoxed about the cause. (OP, Ch. 7)

Flustered - Disturbed, made nervous. Aunt Petunia looks flustered when discussing dementors, whom she had heard about from Lily and James. (OP, Ch. 2) Mrs. Weasley seems flustered with the *austere* manner of Aurors *escorting* Harry and her children to Kings Cross Station. (HBP, Ch. 7)

Foisted - Forced someone to accept. Ernie McMillan says the Ministry has foisted a useless teacher — Dolores Umbridge — on Hogwarts students at a time when they need to learn how to fight dark wizards more than ever. (OP, Ch. 16)

Foraged - Searched about, usually for food. Winky, unlike Dobby, had not foraged for clothes. (GF, Ch. 21)

Foreboding - Feeling that something bad will happen. When Prof. McGonagall calls to Harry amid a crowd of student, he has a sense of foreboding. (PA, Ch. 5) Harry has feeling of foreboding when Uncle Vernon says that when the Weasleys visit, they better be wearing normal clothes. (GF, Ch. 4)

Forestalled - Stopped before something happened. Snape forestalled Bellatrix before she opened her mouth by stating the question she was about to ask. (HBP, Ch. 2)

Forewarned - Warned in advance. When Hermione noticed that Ron's wrote in his Divination homework that he will drown not once but twice, he yawns, "At least I'm forewarned." (GF, Ch. 14) As he prepared to bath in the prefect's bathroom, Harry packed the Marauder's Map so that he could be forewarned of anyone's approach. (GF, Ch. 25)

Forgo — Give up an opportunity. After Snape asks Filch to help him search for an *intruder* who broke into his office, Filch appears *reluctant* to forgo the chance to catch Peeves, whom he suspects of mischief. (GF, Ch. 25)

Forlorn - Sad. After the Bulgarian team lost, their mascots — Veela — look forlorn. (GF, Ch. 8)

Formalized - Made official. The Ministry of Magic's interest in knowing what's happening at Hogwarts is formalized with a decree that names Dolores Umbridge to be Hogwarts High Inquisitor. (OP, Ch. 15)

Formidable - Having qualities that discourage attack and inspire fear or awe. Neville was raised by his grandmother, a formidable witch. (GF, Ch. 10) Dudley becomes even more formidable when he learns how to box. (OP, Ch. 1)

Formulating - Forming. Harry fears that Hogwarts students are formulating their own theories of how Cedric died. (GF, Ch. 37)

Fortified - Strengthened or encouraged. Harry feels fortified by sight of Albus Dumbeldore at Harry's hearing before the Wizengamot. (OP, Ch. 8)

Fortnight - Two weeks. The *prospect* of speaking to Sirius was all that *sustained* Harry during the fortnight before the first task in the Triwizard Tournament. (GF, Ch. 19) Dumbledore rescues Harry from the need to spend more than a fortnight on Privet Drive. (HBP, Ch. 3)

Fractionally - By a small, almost insignificant amount. Ron looks fractionally more cheerful after Harry and Hermione spend most of dinner criticizing the Apparition examiner. (HBP, Ch. 22)

Fraternization - Hanging around together as friends. Percy writes to Ron to warn him about his fraternization with Harry, which Percy considers unwise. (OP, Ch. 14)

Fraternizing - Associating with other people in a friendly or intimate way. When Hermione attends the Yule Ball with Viktor Krum, Ron accuses her of fraternizing with the enemy. (GF, Ch. 23)

Fraught - Full of something that is indicated. Dumbledore says Harry's inheritance of property from Sirius Black is fraught with complications. (HBP, Ch. 3)

Frenzied - Intense, quick. Ron speaks to Harry between frenzied mouthfuls of *gateau*. (HBP, Ch. 8)

Frenzy - Wild, rapid movement or activity. The sight of half-packed trucks put Pigwidgeon into a frenzy of excitement. (GF, Ch. 10)

Fretful - Disturbed. After several visits from Cornelius Fudge, the Prime Minister is quite disturbed to see him emerge from the fireplace once again, looking more *disheveled* and fretful than ever. (HBP, Ch. 1)

Fretfully - Irritably; in a bad mood. Aragog fretfully orders that Harry and Ron be eaten so he can go back to his nap. (CS, Ch. 15)

Frivolous - Silly, lighthearted or unimportant. After Prof. Trelawney catches Harry laughing at her, she says that someone who had seen what she saw in her crystal ball would not be so frivolous. (GF, Ch. 21)

Frothed - Issued foam. The Polyjuice Potion frothed as its ingredients reacted with each other. (CS, Ch. 12)

Fug - A smelly vapor. Harry slept with his glasses *askew*, snoring loudly and leaving a misty *fug* on the window. (HBP, Ch. 3)

Fuming - Stewing in anger. Harry is fuming after Madam Pomfrey refuses to allow him to leave the hospital after a Quidditch injury. (HBP, Ch. 19)

Furled - Folded-up or rolled-up. When Harry first sees his Hungarian Horntail in the Triwizard Tournament, he sees it has its wings half-furled. (GF, Ch. 20)

Furrowed - Marked by narrow depressions. Mr. Weasley reads *The Daily Prophet* with a furrowed *brow*. (PA, Ch. 5)

Furtive - Doing things in a way to avoid notice. Each Ministry of Magic car that transported the Weasleys and Harry to King's Cross was driven by a furtive-looking wizard. (PA, Ch. 5) Classmates shoot furtive glances at Harry after Prof. Trelawney sees a Grim in his teacup, as if he might die at any moment. (PA, Ch. 6) Slughorn gives Harry a furtive look at their first meeting, then comments how he has his mother's eyes. (HBP, Ch. 4)

Gaggle - Bunch. Harry sees a gaggle of young wizards near three veela. (GF, Ch. 9)

Gallant - Brave and gracious. Ludo Bagman calls the Bulgarian Quidditch players gallant after their loss in the Quidditch World Cup. (GF, Ch. 8)

Gamboled - Skipped about in play. As a black dog, Sirius Black gamboled by chasing his own tail. (OP, Ch. 10)

Gateau - Cake, usually with a cream or fruit filling. Ron adores chocolate gateau. (GF, Ch. 12)

Gate-crash - Come to a party uninvited. Malfoy admits he was trying to gate-crash Slughorn's party. (HBP, Ch. 15)

Gaunt - Used to describe the face of a person who has been sick or hasn't eaten enough. Sirius Black's face is repeatedly described as gaunt. (Gaunt also turns out to be the surname — last name — of Voldemort's grandfather.) (PA, Ch. 2)

Gauzy - Sheer, able to be seen through. Prof. Trelawney wears a gauzy shawl. (PA, Ch. 15)

Gawping - In England, gawking. Harry says he'll trade places with Ron anytime, and Ron would see what it's like to have people gawping at your forehead wherever you go. (GF, Ch. 18)

Genially - In a friendly way. Slughorn speaks genially. (HBP, Ch. 9)

Gesticulating - Moving one's hands to call attention to something. Upset with a Quidditch referee's decision to eject their mascots, two Bulgarian players landed next to him and began gesticulating at the Irish mascots. (GF, Ch. 8)

Gesture - An act done in order to convey one's sentiments, such as giving a small gift or sending a card. Bellatrix LeStrange is offended when Snape says that her willingness to go to Azkaban out of loyalty to Voldemort was merely a gesture because the use of that particular word suggests the sacrifice was minor. (HBP, Ch. 2)

Gibbering - Speaking in a disorganized way. Harry finds himself gibbering to a Ministry of Magic examiner after he has a dreamlike experience of hearing Voldemort attacking Sirius. (OP, Ch. 22)

Gist - Key idea of a piece of communication. Although Snape could not hear the names that Harry and Ron called him after he insulted Hermione, Snape got the gist and gave them both detention. (GF, Ch. 18)

Git - In England, a stupid or unpleasant fellow. Fred calls Snape a git behind his back. (OP, Ch. 4)

Glen - A small valley in an out-of-the-way place. The Sorting Hat sings that Gyffindor grew up in a *moor*, Ravenclaw in a glen, Hufflepuff in a valley and Slytherin in a *fen*. (GF, Ch. 12)

Glint - A flash. Describing her plan for using Polyjuice Potion, Hermione has a *steely* glint in her eye that reminds Harry of Prof. McGonagall. (CS, Ch. 12)

Gloat - To take pleasure in another's misfortune, especially if one predicted it. After Harry's secret trip to Hogsmeade ends in disaster, Hermione approaches Harry and Ron, who says, "Come to have a good gloat?" (PA, Ch. 14)

Glowered - Stared with annoyance or anger. Dudley glowered at his mother when she served him unsweetened grapefruit as part of a new diet. (GF, Ch. 3) Viktor Krum glowered when he asked Harry if he and Hermione are dating, as *The Daily Prophet* had reported. (GF, Ch. 28)

Glummest - Saddest. Moaning Myrtle has the glummest face that Harry had ever seen. (CS, Ch. 8)

Glutinous - Gummy. Polyjuice Potion is glutinous. (CS, Ch. 12)

Gnarled - Bent. Upon overhearing the word "Quidditch," Frank Bryce puts a gnarled finger in his ear. (GF, Ch. 1) Mad Eye Moody's hands are gnarled. (GF, Ch. 14) The Snarlgaluff plant looks like a gnarled stump but it shoots out protective, prickly vines. (HBP, Ch. 14)

Goaded - Moved into action by something unpleasant. At his hearing before the Wizengamot, Harry is goaded by Fudge's criticisms and Percy's *sanctimonious* nod of agreement to shout out his side of the story. (OP, Ch. 8)

Gormless - In England, stupid. Mundungus Fletcher tells a story of how he sold toads to a gormless gargoyle, stole them away from him, and then sold them back at twice the original price. (OP, Ch. 5) Ron looks gormless in potions class when he and Harry try to figure what Golpalott's Third Law means. (HBP, Ch. 18)

Gouge - Dig. Harry notices that when the Hungarian Horntail thrashes its spiked tail, it leaves gouge marks in the ground. (GF, Ch. 20)

Grappled - Fought. Copies of the Monster Book of Monsters grapple with each other at Flourish and Blotts bookstore. (PA, Ch. 4)

Gratitude - Thankfulness. Hedwig is furious at Harry's lack of gratitude for delivering a message. (GF, Ch. 15)

Gravely - Seriously. When Hermione asks Hagrid to join S.P.E.W., he says gravely, "It'd be doing them an unkindness." (GF, Ch. 16)

Dumbledore gravely tells Harry not to jump to conclusions about his grades. (HBP, Ch. 4)

Graver - More serious. The Prime Minister thinks that he and Fudge have been seeing rather a lot of each other, and he worries that on his next visit Fudge will bring still graver news. (HBP, Ch. 1)

Grievous - Serious, bad. Ron is *affronted* when a healer in a portrait at St. Mungos calls out that he clearly has a most grievous skin sickness called "spattergroit." (OP, Ch. 23)

Grim - Fierce, determined. Before a Quidditch match, Snape wears a grim smile. (PA, Ch. 15)

Grimace - Facial expression showing disgust. Uncle Vernon smiles for the neighbors but his expression turns into a grimace when he speaks to Harry. (OP, Ch. 1)

Grisly - Gross, inspiring horror. Snape personalizes his classroom by putting up *gruesome* pictures of people with grisly injuries or strangely *contorted* body parts. (HBP, Ch. 9)

Grizzled - Gray. Mad-Eye Moody has a long *mane* of grizzled hair. (GF, Ch. 14)

Groggy - Sleepy, not paying attention. Ron looks groggy while Ginny and Mrs. Weasly whisper about Fleur Delacour. (HBP, Ch. 5)

Groped - Moved unsteadily, as in darkness. Frank Bryce groped his way through the Riddle house before encountering Nagini. (GF, Ch. 1)

Grotesque - Gross, ugly. Harry sees four figures in the air, being *contorted* into grotesque shapes by dark wizards on the ground. (GF, Ch. 9) Malfoy makes a grotesque face as he tells Ron that his father is destined for a St. Mungo's ward that serves people whose brains have been *addled* by magic - a comment that upsets Neville greatly. (OP, Ch. 17) After Fenrir Greyback bites Bill, his injured face is grotesque. (HBP, Ch. 29)

Grudgingly - With reluctance. Although Aunt Petunia took Harry into her home grudgingly, but even though she didn't love him, an ancient magic involving family love protected Harry. (OP, Ch. 37)

Grueling - Difficult, punishing, exhausting. The Prime Minister convinced himself that Fudge was a *hallucination* brought about by his exhaustion after his grueling campaign for office. (HBP, Ch. 1)

Gruesome - Gross, inspiring horror. Snape personalized his classroom by putting up gruesome pictures of people with *grisly* injuries or strangely *contorted* body parts. (HBP, Ch. 9)

Guffaw - A burst of laughter. With a guffaw, Moaning Myrtle tells Hermione, "Wait till everyone finds out you've got a tail!" (CS, Ch. 13)

Hags - Ugly witches. Harry thinks that hags prefer to live in Hogsmeade, an all-wizard village, because they are not good at disguising themselves as Muggles. (GF, Ch. 19)

Hallucination - False perception of reality brought about by mental illness. The Prime Minister convinced himself that Fudge was a hallucination brought about by his exhaustion after his grueling campaign for office. (HBP, Ch. 1)

Hampered - Held back. Harry and Ron want to follow the spiders, as Hagrid suggested, but are hampered by rules that forbid students from wandering the grounds. (CS, Ch. 15)

Hardened - Devoted to a path of crime or anti-social behavior. Children on Privet Drive had been warned that Harry was a hardened hooligan who attends St. Brutus's Secure Center for Incurably Criminal Boys. (OP, Ch. 1)

Harebrained - Nutty. Harry feared that Hagrid had some harebrained scheme that would keep him from meeting Sirius on time. (GF, Ch. 19)

Harping - Dwelling on a subject so much that it annoys others. Harry warns Hermione to stop harping on the Half-Blood Prince's copy of *Advanced Potion Making*. (HBP, Ch. 24)

Haughtily - With an air of superiority. Buckbeak eyed Harry haughtily, at first. (PA, Ch. 6) Hermione ends a conversation haughtily after Ron expresses doubt that she has figured out why Lupin disappears every month. (PA, Ch. 11) Prof. McGonagall answers Umbridge's questions haughtily. (OP, Ch. 29)

Haughty - Proud, with an air of superiority. Prof. Trelawney stood up straight and looked haughty as she confessed that Dumbledore had requested fewer visits from her. (HBP, Ch. 25)

Haven - Safe and comfortable place. Hogsmeade was the only all-wizard village in Britain, and Harry supposed it was a haven for *hags*, who were not *adept* at disguising themselves as Muggles. (GF, Ch. 19)

Havoc - Destruction or confusion. Peeves is described as "a grinning, *airborne* menace who lived to cause havoc and distress." (CS, Ch. 8)

Heartily - With enjoyment and enthusiasm. Wood heartily urges his teammates to grab their brooms and being training. (CS, Ch. 7) After Mad-Eye Moody turns Draco Malfoy into a ferret, Hermione teases him about the incident and them laughs heartily along with Harry and Ron. (GF, Ch. 23)

Heatedly - With anger. Fudge responds heatedly when the Prime Minister suggests he has not made a sufficient effort to capture Lord Voldemort. (HBP, Ch. 1)

Heightened - Raised. Harry's feeling of embarrassment was heightened by his memory of how poorly he behaved in Dumbledore's office. (HBP, Ch. 4)

Heinous - Shockingly evil. Barty Crouch calls his son's acts heinous before sentencing him to Azkaban. (GF, Ch. 30)

Heir (pronounced "air") - One who inherits from an ancestor. Fred and George thought the idea that Harry was Slytherin's heir was *ludicrous*. (CS, Ch. 12)

Heirloom - Family treasure. Dumbledore says Merope sold a family heirloom to Caractacus Burke. (HBP, Ch. 13) Morphin lived his last days in Azkaban, *lamenting* the loss of Marvolo's heirloom. (HBP, Ch. 17)

Henchmen - Evil assistants. Dumbledore asks Voldemort why he came back to Hogwarts with loyal henchmen waiting for him in a tavern. (HBP, Ch. 20)

Highflier - Person of talent and achievement. Molly Weasley says Slughorn took much interest in Arthur because the professor did not perceive Arthur to be enough of a highflier. (HBP, Ch 5)

Hillock - A small hill. Harry sees green tents at the Quidditch World Cup that look like hillocks. (GF, Ch. 7)

Hindrance - Someone or something that interferes with the accomplishment of a goal. Mr. Weasley was more of hindrance than a help in assembling tents at the Quidditch World Cup, because he got overexcited about using a *mallet*. (GF, Ch. 7)

Hitherto - Until now. A double attack on Justin and Nearly Headless Nick turns "what had hitherto been nervousness" into real panic. (CS, Ch. 12) Fred says with a yawn that he supposed that when Ron turns 16 he will "dazzle us all with hitherto unsuspected magical skills." (HBP, Ch. 16)

Hoarse - Rough-sounding. The Gryffindor fans were screaming themselves hoarse. (PA, Ch. 15)

Hobbled - Moved with a limp. Filch hobbled across his office to snatch his Kwikspell letter out of Harry's sight. (CS, Ch. 8)

Hoisted - Lifted up. After their victory over Slytherin, the Gryffindor Quidditch team was hoisted onto the shoulders of the crowd.

Honed - Crafted. The Firebolt is described as "honed to *aerodynamic* perfection." (PA, Ch. 4)

Hoodwinks - Tricks, fools or gets away with a lie. Dumbledore says he will make sure that no Hogwarts student under 17 years old hoodwinks the *impartial* judge into selecting him or her as Hogwarts Champion.

(GF, Ch. 12) Snape mocks Bellatrix by asking if she thinks he had hood-winked the Dark Lord. (HBP, Ch. 2)

Hooligan - A bully or violent lawbreaker. Children on Privet Drive had been warned that Harry was a *hardened* hooligan who attends St. Brutus's Secure Center for Incurably Criminal Boys. (OP, Ch. 1)

Horrific - Horrible. Rita Skeeter writes that Hagrid has been subjecting his students to a *succession* of horrific creatures in his class at Hogwarts. (GF, Ch. 24)

Hovel - A hut or tiny house, usually poorly maintained. Malfoy says the Weasleys live in a hovel. (OP, Ch. 19)

Humiliation - State of extreme embarrassment. Malfoy endures the humiliation of being turned into a ferret by Prof. Moody. (GF, Ch. 13)

Hurtled - Moved very fast, with a rushing sound. In Gringotts Bank, carts hurtle down tracks through a maze of twisty passages. (SS, Ch. 6)

Huskily - In a choked-up voice. Hagrid calls for Buckbeak huskily when he suddenly disappears just before he is supposed to be executed. (PA, Ch. 20)

Hygienic - Clean. Dumbledore informs Harry that Fred and George sent him a toilet seat, but that Madam Pomfrey *confiscated* it because it was not very hygienic. (SS, Ch. 17)

Hypocrite - Someone who says one thing but does another. Ginny calls Ron a hypocrite because he kisses a girl at a party after criticizing Ginny for similar behavior with her boyfriend Dean Thomas. (HBP, Ch. 14)

Hypothetical - Based on an assumption or conjecture. When Tom Riddle asks Slughorn about Horcruxes, Slughorn seeks Riddle's assurance that the discussion is hypothetical rather than something Riddle would ever try to do. (HBP, Ch. 23)

Hysteria - State of extreme worry or agitation. Hermione thinks all the hysteria over giants is just *prejudice* and *bigotry*. (GF, Ch. 24) With a note of hysteria in her voice, Narcissa Malfoy threatens her sister Bellatrix with her wand. (HBP, Ch. 2)

Hysterical - When Ron makes a mildly funny remark about Goyle, Luna Lovegood reacts with *prolonged* laughter, as if the comment was hysterical. (OP, Ch. 10)

Hysterics - Sobbing and emotional distress. In anticipation of arrival of delegations from Beaubatons and Durmstrang, Argus Flich put pair of first-year girls into hysterics with his obsession about cleanliness. (GF, Ch. 15)

Ignorant - Unknowing, uninformed. The Prime Minister did not like Fudge's visits because Fudge often spoke of unfamiliar things and made him feel like an ignorant schoolboy. (HBP, Ch. 1) Voldemort tells Dumbledore that he is woefully ignorant of some kinds of magic. (HBP, Ch. 20)

Illustrious - Famed, notable for achievements. Slughorn is full of *anecdotes* about illustrious wizards he has known. (HBP, Ch. 7)

Imbues - Penetrates and adds a quality. Dragons are born with an ancient magic that imbues their hides with a protection against all but the most powerful of spells. (GF, Ch. 20)

Immense - Extreme or large. Harry folded up a note to Ron with immense difficulty so it would fit in Errol's tiny leg. (GF, Ch. 3) The stadium at the Quidditch World Cup is immense. (GF, Ch. 8) Dobby's eyes are immense. (GF, Ch. 21)

Immensely - Extremely. Percy looks immensely proud and important when he is put in charge. (PA, Ch. 9) Human transfiguration is an immensely difficult topic. (HBP, Ch. 15)

Immersed - Fully interested in something; absorbed. Harry is not surprised to see Hermione immersed in the *Standard Book of Spells*. (GF, Ch. 10) Dumbledore says he believes that Voldemort is so immersed in evil that he no longer feels the way human beings do. (HBP, Ch. 23)

Imminent - About to occur. The imminent arrival of the Weasleys had the Dursley's very nervous and irritable. (GF, Ch. 4) A ugly little man in a painting warns the Prime Minister about the imminent arrival of Cornelius Fudge. (HBP, Ch. 1)

Immobilized - Frozen, unable to move. Mrs. Weasley follows instructions in a book by Gilderoy Lockhart to immobilize doxies. (OP, Ch. 6) Harry is immobilized by Malfoy on the Hogwarts Express. (HBP, Ch. 7)

Immortality - State of living forever. Dumbledore says that many looking into the Mirror of Erised would have seen themselves acquiring immortality or riches. (HBP, Ch. 23)

Immovable - Unable to be moved. Harry didn't know Dumbledore's password, so the gargoyle that guarded his office was immovable. (GF, Ch. 29)

Impaled - Stuck with a sharp object. After Gilderoy Lockhart's memory-erasing charm backfires, Dumbledore says, "Impaled on your own sword, Gilderoy!" Dumbledore was using the image of being injured with one's own sword to say that Lockhart would not have ended up being hurt had he not tried to hurt others. (CS, Ch. 18)

Impartial - Evenhanded, without any reason to favor one of several competitors. The Goblet of Fire is an impartial judge used to decide which students should represent their schools in the Triwizard Tournament. (GF, Ch. 16)

Impassively - Without emotion. Firenze looked at Harry impassively when he told him to warn Hagrid that an attempt he was making (to tame a giant, we later learn) is not working. (OP, Ch. 27)

Impeccably - Perfectly, without flaw. When Harry first sees Barty Crouch, he is dressed impeccably in a suit and tie. (GF, Ch. 7)

Impeded - Held back. Harry and the Weasleys find their progress impeded by a crowd of wizards at the edge of the forest near the site of the Quidditch World Cup. (GF, Ch. 9)

Impenetrable - Unable to be entered. Outside the Room of Requirement is a stretch of stone that appears impenetrable. (HBP, Ch. 25)

Imperceptibly - Subtly or slightly, so as to be undetectable. As Snape begins to convince Bellatrix of his loyalty to the Dark Lord, she nods very slightly, almost imperceptibly. (HBP, Ch. 2)

Imperiously - Commanding. Madame Maxine imperiously asks Dumbledore to explain how Harry was selected by the Goblet of Fire. (GF, Ch. 17) Buckbeak looks at Harry, Ron and Hermione imperiously before bowing. (GF, Ch. 27) Hedwig looks around Harry's room at Privet Drive imperiously. (HBP, Ch. 3) Hepzibah speaks imperiously to her house elf, Hokey. (HBP, Ch. 20)

Impersonal - Businesslike. Firenze says centaurs look upon the heavens in an impersonal and *impartial* way. (OP, Ch. 27)

Impersonated - Imitated. In a Muggle house, Harry sits in a chair much like the one that Slughorn had just impersonated. (HBP, Ch. 4) Arthur Weasley wants to be sure Molly is not actually a Death Eater who is impersonating his wife, so he asks her to say her nickname. (HBP, Ch. 5)

Impersonation - Imitation. Fred does a great impersonation of Percy. (PA, Ch. 10)

Impertinent - Disrespectful. When Harry demands information from Phineas Nigellus Black, the image in the portrait raises an eyebrow, as if he found Harry impertinent. (OP, Ch. 23) Phineas calls Harry impertinent a year later. (HBP, Ch. 13)

Implicitly - Unstated; can also mean absolutely and without doubt. Bellatrix LeStrange asks Snape whether Dumbledore has any suspicions about his true allegiance and asks, "He trusts you implicitly still?" (HBP, Ch. 2)

Imploringly - In a manner close to begging. As Hermione tries to explain Sirius Black's innocence to Cornelius Fudge, she looks at his face imploringly. (PA, Ch. 20)

Importing - Bringing into the country. Cornelius Fudge advises the Prime Minister that wizards are importing three dragons and a sphinx into the country. (HBP, Ch. 1)

Imposter - One who pretends to be another person or claims to have a role of authority that he or she is not entitled to. Dumbledore tells Harry that he should ask him his favorite flavor of jam to make sure that he is not an imposter. (HBP, Ch. 4)

Imprecations - Curses. Ron is so upset that Ginny is dating Michael Corner that he *chunters* and utters imprecations under his breath. (OP, Ch. 16)

Impregnable - Unable to be entered or penetrated. When Ron agreed with Harry that they were both going to get a date for the Yule Ball by day's end, his tone suggested they were planning to storm an impregnable fortress. (GF, Ch. 22)

Impressive - Causing others to admire or have other strong reaction. Sir Nicholas asks Harry to tell another ghost how frightening and impressive he finds the Gryffindor House ghost. (CS, Ch. 8)

Imprint - Left over image. A ghost is the imprint of a departed soul, Snape says. (HBP, Ch. 21)

In due course - Later, at the proper time. Dumbledore promises to tell Harry about his whereabouts over the prior weekend "in due course." (HBP, Ch. 13)

Inadvertently - Accidentally. Dumbledore tells the young Tom Riddle that he is aware that Tom has been using magic in an improper way — "inadvertently, I am sure." (HBP, Ch. 13)

Inadvisable - Not wise or recommended. Snape tells Harry that Dumbledore believes it inadvisable for Voldemort to continue to penetrate Harry's mind in dreams, which is why Harry must learn to shut his mind through Occlumency. (OP, Ch. 24) Dumbledore says it's possible to make a Horcrux out of a live animal, such as a snake, but it is inadvisable to do so because the snake can make its own decisions. (HBP, Ch. 23)

Inaudible - Unable to be heard. After Harry used a bezoar to save Ron's life, Hermione gave an almost inaudible sniff. (HBP, Ch. 19)

Incantation - Magic words. Hermione tells Fudge she heard an incantation spoken just before the Dark Mark appeared in the sky. (GF, Ch. 9)

Incautious - Not careful. Snape tells Malfoy that he is being incautious by wandering around at night. (HBP, Ch. 15)

Incensed - Angered. Lucius Malfoy gives an incensed stare to Harry and the newly freed Dobby before he leaves Hogwarts. (CS, Ch. 18) Harry is incensed when his potion sample drops to the floor and Snape gives him a zero. (OP, Ch. 29)

Incessantly - All the time. Pidwidgeon is so excited about being called upon to make a delivery that he flew around and around Harry's head, hooting incessantly. (GF, Ch. 21)

Inclination - Tendency to do something. Snape says Harry has shown little inclination to follow school rules. (OP, Ch. 32)

Inclined - Tilted. Snape inclined his head and drank a toast to Bellatrix LeStrange in honor of her role in the death of Sirius Black. (HBP, Ch. 2)

Incoherently - Unable to be understood. After Voldemort accuses of him of wanting to abandon him, Wormtail speaks incoherently. (GF, Ch. 1)

Incomparable - Unique. Dumbledore says the power of an *untarnished* soul like Harry's is incomparable. (HBP, Ch. 23)

Incomprehensible - Unable to be understood. Neville's speech is incomprehensible after Harry drags him away from a fight with Malfoy. (OP, Ch. 17) Harry finds the egg in the Triwizard Tournament incomprehensible, and his *conscience* bothers him because he misled Hagrid into thinking he had made progress with it. (GF, Ch. 24)

Inconsistent - Not steady, varying. Harry knew Ron was an inconsistent Quidditch goalkeeper. (HBP, Ch. 14)

Incorporates - Includes. The Firebolt incorporates an "unbreakable Braking Charm." (PA, Ch. 4)

Incredulity - State of disbelief. Neville has a look of incredulity when Prof. McGonagall tells him his grandmother failed her Charms OWL. (HBP, Ch. 9)

Incredulously - In a doubting way. Harry and Ron look incredulously at Hermione when she explains her plan for using Polyjuice Potion (CS, Ch. 12) Fred stares incredulously at the letter saying Ron has been named a prefect. (OP, Ch. 9) When Dumbledore says he does not think a conversation involving Snape and Malfoy that Harry overhead is of great importance, Harry repeats Dumbledore's comment incredulously. (HBP, Ch. 17)

Incriminated - Cast suspicion on someone about a crime or improper act. The facts about how Harry came to possess the Marauder's Map incriminated Fred and George Weasley, among others. (GF, Ch. 25)

Incriminating - Casting suspicion on someone about a crime or improper act. Dumbledore says Lucius Malfoy slipped Tom Riddle's diary to Ginny Weasley in an effort to discredit Arthur Weasley and get rid of an incriminating object at the same time. (HBP, Ch. 23)

Incumbent - Obliged to perform a duty. Harry felt it incumbent upon him to tell Sirius that he should not risk himself despite Snape's taunts about being no help to the Order. (OP, Ch. 24)

Incurably - Hopelessly. Harry tells Aunt Marge that he attends not Hogwarts but "St. Brutus's Secure Center for Incurably Criminal Boys."

(GF, Ch. 2) Prof. Lockhart is remembered by Harry as incurably inept. (HBP, Ch. 19)

Incursion - Hostile penetration. Snape said a vision that Harry had before Christmas represented a powerful incursion into Voldemort's thoughts, but is interrupted by Harry before he can explain there is risk of the reverse taking place. (OP, Ch. 24)

Indecent - Improper, not fit for public view. Snape looked away from Narcissa Malfoy's tears as if they were indecent. (HBP, Ch. 2)

Indifferently - Neutrally, without preference. Bellatrix Lestrange responds indifferently to Narcissa Malfoy's worries about Draco dying, saying it would still be a good thing if it happens in service to the Dark Lord. (HBP, Ch. 2) Zabini responds indifferently when Malfoy wonders why Neville was invited to the Slug Club. (HBP, Ch. 7)

Indignantly - With a sense of outrage. Hedwig shrieks indignantly when the entrance to platform 9 3/4 suddenly seals up and the owl's cage falls from Harry's trolley, hitting the ground. (CS, Ch. 5) Ginny says her brother Fred's name indignantly after he tells Ron that Scabbers is probably better off dead. (PA, Ch. 13) Hermione speaks indignantly when she finds out Harry has still not figured out the egg clue, even though he had said he had. (GF, Ch. 26)

Indignation - Outrage. Prof. Lupin smiles at the look of indignation on his students' faces when they tell him that Snape had ordered them to write a long essay about werewolves. (PA, Ch. 10)

Indignity - State of being insulted or held up to ridicule. Prof. Trelawney complains about the indignity of being evaluated by Dolores Umbridge. (OP, Ch. 17)

Indigo - Dark blue. Looking up from his hospital bed, Harry sees a sky streaked with indigo and *crimson* and realizes the Quidditch match ended a long time ago. (HBP, Ch. 19)

Indiscriminately - Wildly, not aiming. Harry sees Morfin firing hexes indiscriminately. (HBP, Ch. 10)

Indisposed - Unavailable. When Harry asks why Hagrid wasn't present at a Care of Magical Creatures class, Prof. Grubbly-Plank says vaguely, "He is indisposed." (GF, Ch. 24)

Indistinctly - Unclearly. When awoken by his mother, Ron mutters some words indistinctly. (GF, Ch. 6)

Indistinguishable - Exactly the same. After drinking Polyjuice Potion, Ron is indistinguishable from Crabbe. (CS, Ch. 12)

Induce - Cause to occur. Malfoy pretends to know a key examiner from the Ministry of Magic just to induce panic among the Gryffindors. (OP, Ch. 21)

Ineptitude - Poor skill. Harry knows that lots of bangs and smoke are signs of ineptitude in a wizard. (HBP, Ch. 26)

Inexorably - Happening relentlessly and with certainty. Harry finds himself on a boat with Dumbledore that sails inexorably toward a hiding place of one of Voldemort's Horcruxes. (HBP, Ch. 26)

Inexpertly - In a mediocre style. Harry sees wizard who are dressed in Muggle clothes, but inexpertly; one wizard had on a kilt and a poncho. (GF, Ch. 7)

Inexplicable - Unable to be explained. Hermione acted *oblivious* to the tension between Ron and Lavender, but Harry notices an inexplicable smirk on her face. (HBP, Ch. 20)

Inexplicably - Without explanation. Hermione smiles inexplicably when she takes Harry's glasses, but Harry understands why after she casts a spell that protects the glasses from rain. (PA, Ch. 9)

Inextricably - Pertaining to something that cannot be untied or untangled. For some reason, Harry thought his chances to date Ginny and the outcome of a Quidditch match were inextricably linked. (HBP, Ch. 24)

Infamous - Famous for being bad. *The Daily Prophet* describes Sirius Black as "the most infamous prisoner ever to be held in Azkaban." (PA, Ch. 3)

Infectious - Easy to share or join in. At the Quidditch World Cup, the atmosphere of excitement was infectious. (GF, Ch. 8)

Infernal - Awful, like something you'd find in hell. After visiting vault 713 in Gringotts, Hagrid tells Harry, "Come on, back in this infernal cart, and don't talk to me on the way back, it's best if I keep me mouth shut." (SS, Ch. 5)

Infinite - Without end. After drinking Felix Felicis, Harry feels an "an *exhilarating* sense of infinite opportunity." (HBP, Ch. 22)

Inflection - Tone of voice. With a nasty inflection in his voice, Bane asked another centaur what he thought they should do with Hagrid, who had returned to the Forbidden Forest despite warnings. (OP, Ch. 30)

Inflexible - Unwilling to change one's mind. Harry thinks of Prof. McGonagall as *irascible* and inflexible. (OP, Ch. 32)

Infuriating - Angering. George congratulated Ron on infuriating Percy. (PA, Ch. 5) The Prime Minister found it infuriating to learn that wizards were involved in a bridge collapse because he couldn't tell anyone. (HBP, Ch. 1)

Ingenious - Brilliant, imaginative. Mr. Weasley describes automatic ticket machines in the London Underground (subway) as ingenious. (OP, Ch. 6) Dumbledore says Slughorn's method of gaining access to Muggle houses is ingenious. (HBP, Ch. 4) When Draco tells Dumbledore that he found a way to allow Death Eaters into Hogwarts, Dumbledore says, "Ingenious." (HBP, Ch. 27)

Ingenuity - Cleverness. Dumbledore asks Harry to use all his ingenuity to pry an important memory out of Slughorn. (HBP, Ch. 20)

Ingratiating - Getting on someone's good side. Hagrid attempts an ingratiating smile when Dolores Umbridge demands to know why, if he had been to the South of France as he claimed, he had no tan. (OP, Ch. 20)

Inhabitants - Residents. The inhabitants of Little Hangleton tell tales of what happened in the Riddle house, often *embroidering* the tale. (GF, Ch. 1)

Inherit - To be left something when someone dies. Dumbledore tells Harry, "you inherit all of Sirius' *possessions*." (HBP, Ch. 3)

Initial - Occurring first or early on. Snape says Voldemort's initial *displeasure* with him evaporated once he realized how useful Snape could be to him as a spy. (HBP, Ch. 2)

Injust - Unfair. Madame Maxine says that it would be most injust for Hogwarts to have two champions. (GF, Ch. 17)

Inkling - A slight, early sense of knowing something. Harry had an inkling that a romance might develop between Ron and Hermione at some point. (HBP, Ch. 14)

Innumerable - Too many to count. In the Great Hall, innumerable candles hovered in midair. (CS, Ch. 5)

Inquisitorial - Intensely questioning. At Tom Riddle's orphanage, Mrs. Cole shoots an inquisitorial glance at Dumbledore to be sure that he intends to take Tom with him no matter what she reveals about him. (HBP, Ch. 13)

Inscrutable - Hard to read. Snape's face is inscrutable. (HBP, Ch. 15)

Inscrutably - In a way that's hard to understand. Crookshanks stares inscrutably at Harry. (GF, Ch. 14)

Insinuations - Sly remarks that suggest negative things about a person. Prof. Trelawney says Dolores Umbridge's inspection report make insinuations about her that she finds insulting. (OP, Ch. 17)

Insolent - Disrespectful. Aunt Marge calls Harry insolent when he challenges her insulting statements about his parents. (PA, Ch. 2) Malfoy gives Lupin an insolent stare. (PA, Ch. 6)

Insubstantial - Weak or lacking substance. At 12 Grimmauld Place, rooms are lit by insubstantial light. (OP, Ch. 4)

Insufferable - Awful, unbearable. Snape calls Hermione "an insufferable know-it-all." (PA, Ch. 9)

Insurmountable - Impossible to conquer. The problem of how to get to the Ministry of Magic to rescue Sirius seems insurmountable. (OP, Ch. 33)

Intensified - Grew stronger. Harry thinks Snape's hatred of him intensified after Harry helped Sirius Black escape "right under Snape's overlarge nose." (GF, Ch. 12)

Intermingle - Mix together. Prof. Trelawney says you can tell the future by looking at stars and the planets, whose rays intermingle in the night sky. (GF, Ch. 13)

Interrogated - Questioned intensely, like a police investigator. Harry tries to ask Aunt Petunia about the strange howler she got from Harry's dead mother, but she is so tight-lipped that "he might as well have interrogated a doorknob." (OP, Ch. 3) Ernie McMillian interrogated people about their study habits. (OP, Ch. 21) Hermione says everyone on the Hogwarts Express was interrogating her about what happened in the Ministry of Magic. (HBP, Ch. 8)

Interspersed - Mixed in. While flying toward a city with members of the Order of the Phoenix, Harry sees lines of light interspersed with patches of the deepest black. (OP, Ch. 3)

Intervals - Spaces or segments of time of equal length. By checking the Marauder's Map at *strategic* intervals, Harry could be sure that no one was approaching the prefect's bathroom when he tested Cedric's suggestion about solving the riddle of the egg. (GF, Ch. 25)

Intervened - Took action about a situation. In Snape's pensieve, Harry sees that Lily, his mother, intervened when James Potter was teasing Severus Snape. (OP, Ch. 29)

Intimidating - Inspiring meekness in others. When the centaur Firenze begins teaching at Hogwarts, Harry notices that other students seem to find him intimidating. (OP, Ch. 27)

Intimidation - State of cooperation inspired by fear. Rita Skeeter writes that Hagrid plans to continue his *campaign* of intimidation by forcing students to care for blast-ended skrewts. (GF, Ch. 24)

Intolerable - Unbearable. Dumbledore says Voldemort would find dependence on an elixir to be intolerable. (HBP, Ch. 23)

Intrigued - Highly interested, curious. Dumbledore says he was intrigued by Tom Riddle when he enrolled in Hogwarts. (HBP, Ch. 13)

Intruders - Unwelcome guests; those who have gain access to a location by force or trickery. Hedwig regarded *tropical* birds sent by Sirius as intruders. (GF, Ch. 2) Snape insists that Filch help him search for an intruder who broke into his office rather than go up a staircase (where Harry is hidden under his invisibility cloak). (GF, Ch. 25)

Intruding - Breaking in. Harry's unpleasant memory of his behavior during his last *encounter* with Dumbledore kept intruding on his thoughts. (HBP, Ch. 4)

Invaluable - Valuable beyond measure. Voldemort says the information he obtained from Bertha Jorkins was invaluable. (GF, Ch. 1)

Invariably - Always. Whenever Harry worries about Sirius, he invariably slides off his bed and begins pacing. (OP, Ch. 3)

Invincible - Unable to be defeated. Dumbledore says he arranged for Harry to be raised by Muggles because he knew that no spell to protect Harry in the wizarding world would have been invincible if Voldemort returned to full power.
(OP, Ch. 37)

Involuntarily - In a manner that is against one's will or beyond one's control. When Harry says Voldemort's name, Terry Boot gives an involuntary twitch. (OP, Ch. 16) Draco Malfoy's mouth *contorted* involuntarily when Dumbledore pointed out that he had several minutes to kill him but had not done so. (HBP, Ch. 27)

Irascible - Easily provoke to anger or harshness. Harry thinks of Prof. McGonagall as irascible and *inflexible*. (OP, Ch. 32)

Irksome - Bothersome. Harry finds it irksome that teachers are walking students from class to class. (CS, Ch. 15)

Ironic - At odds with the circumstances, sometimes in a funny way. After Snape says he cannot help Umbridge interrogate Harry, he gives her an ironic bow (as if he were a loyal servant) and turns to leave. (OP, Ch. 32)

Irresolute - Undecided. Just before a Quidditch match, Harry briefly hears a voice saying it wants to kill, and he stands, irresolute, not knowing whether he should skip the match in order to investigate this strange occurrence. (CS, Ch. 15) Harry stands irresolute just before sending a patronus against the dementors. (PA, Ch. 20)

Irretrievable - Unable to be recovered, final. Harry refuses to tell Phineas Nigellus that Sirius is dead because speaking that truth would make the death feel irretrievable to Harry. (OP, Ch. 36)

Irritable - In a bad mood. After Sirius Black's escape, Cornelius Fudge is described by *The Daily Prophet* as irritable. (PA, Ch. 3) Harry feels bad about being irritable with Hedwig, who was his only friend on Privet Drive. (OP, Ch. 3)

Isolated - Unusual, not part of a pattern. The Prime Minister hears Cornelius Fudge tell him that an appearance of a disturbing mark at the "Kwidditch" World Cup was an isolated incident. (HBP, Ch. 1)

Isolation - Separation from. While staying on Privet Drive, Harry hates his isolation from news of the wizarding world. (GF, Ch. 5)

Jauntily - In a jaunty manner. After Peter Pettigrew is captured and the group leaves the Shrieking Shack, Crookshanks holds his tail up jauntily. (PA, Ch. 21)

Jaunty - Stylish, lively. Gilderoy Lockhart wears a pointed wizard's hat at jaunty angle. (CS, Ch. 4)

Jest - Joke. When Harry tries to talk his way out of being attacked by Bellatrix Lestrange by mentioning a prophecy, Bellatrix replies, "You jest." (OP, Ch. 35)

Jibe - A humorous insult or teasing remark. Ron ignores a jibe that Hermione makes about his attraction to Madam Rosmerta. (HBP, Ch. 12)

Jocularly - In joking way. Slughorn jocularly attributed Harry's declining performance in potions to his being lovesick (HBP, Ch. 25)

Jovially - Happily. Gilderoy Lockhart greets Harry jovially in the corridor: "We meet again, Harry!" (CS, Ch. 6)

Jubilant - Incredibly happy. Harry senses that Voldemort is jubilant and later reads in *The Daily Prophet* that 10 Death Eaters have escaped from Azkaban. (OP, Ch. 24) After a Quidditch win over Hufflepuff, players from Gryffindor are jubilant. (HBP, Ch. 14) Katie Bell's friends are jubilant after she is released from St. Mungo's. (HBP, Ch. 24)

Juncture - Critical moment. Harry cannot believe that Hermione's love of enforcing rules left her at the juncture when she overhead girls planning to use love potions. (HBP, Ch. 15)

Kip - In England, to sleep in a place that is not one's home. Ron says he would give Viktor Krum his bed and kip on camp bed. (GF, Ch. 16)

Kippers - A kind of fish served smoked. At breakfast, Harry saw tables *laden* with *tureens* of porridge, plates of kippers, mountains of toast, and dishes of eggs and bacon. (CS, Ch. 6)

Klaxonlike - Having a sound like an official warning horn. When Harry and Ron try to enter the girl's dormitory, there is a klaxonlike wailing sound and the steps melt together to make a long, smooth slide. (OP, Ch. 17)

Knave - Jack (in cards); also, a man of humble birth or a trickster. Harry hides and overhears Prof. Trelawney reading cards: "Knave of spades: a dark young man, possibly troubled, one who dislikes the questioner..." (HBP, Ch. 10) Sir Cadogan accuses Harry, Ron and Hermione of being knaves who have come to laugh at him until he learns they want his help. (PA, Ch. 6)

Knickerbockers - Loose-fitting short pants; also the name of the New York City professional basketball team, named after early Dutch settlers of New York who wore such pants. The Dursleys have troubled finding knickerbockers in Dudley's size. (GF, Ch. 3)

Knotgrass - Grass with jointed stems. Hermione uses knotgrass when brewing Polyjuice Potion. (CS, Ch. 11)

Knottiest - Hardest to figure out. Hermione asks the "knottiest question": whether she, Harry and Ron should ask Hagrid about opening the Chamber of Secrets. (CS, Ch. 14)

Labyrinth - Maze. Narcissa Malfoy finds Severus Snape's home in a labyrinth of *dilapidated* buildings in an area that Bellatrix LeStrange calls a "Muggle *dunghill*." (HBP, Ch. 2)

Labyrinthine - Mazelike. Ron and Harry, transformed into Crabbe and Goyle, found the labyrinthine passages of Hogwarts deserted as they searched for the Slytherin common room. (CS, Ch. 12)

Lacewings - An insect with wings and large eyes. One of the ingredients of Polyjuice Potion is lacewings. (CS, Ch. 12)

Laden - Holding or carrying. At breakfast, Harry sees tables laden with *tureens* of porridge, plates of *kippers*, mountains of toast, and dishes of eggs and bacon. (CS, Ch. 6) Ron, suspecting the Polyjuice Potion plan will go wrong, looks at Harry with a "*doom*-laden expression." (CS, Ch. 12)

Lamentable - Awful, regrettable. Snape says Harry is a lamentable potions-maker because he lacks *subtlety*, the ability to sense fine *distinctions*. (OP, Ch. 24)

Lamenting - Regretting, sadly remembering. Morphin lived his last days in Azkaban, lamenting the loss of Marvolo's *heirloom*. (HBP, Ch. 17)

Languidly - Slowly, as if one was under water. Harry languidly removes his coat just before an owl gives him a copy of the Quibbler with his interview. (OP, Ch. 26)

Lank - Long and limp. Moaning Myrtle has lank hair. (CS, Ch. 8)

Lax - Loose, negligent. Rita Skeeter writes in *The Daily Prophet* that there was "lax security" at the Quidditch World Cup before the appearance of the Dark Mark. (GF, Ch. 10)

Layabout - Lazy person. Uncle Vernon calls Sirius Black a "filthy layabout" because a picture of him shows long, messy hair. (PA, Ch. 2)

Leaflet - A folded piece of paper printed with a message and given away free. A purple leaflet in Harry's trunk is emblazoned with the words "Ministry of Magic" and gives safety instructions. (HBP, Ch. 3)

Leer - An unkind look. When Voldemort smiles, it comes across as a leer. (HBP, Ch. 20)

Lest - Or else. The mermaids and mermen sing to Harry, "Your times' half-gone, so tarry not/Lest what you seek stays here to rot." (GF, Ch. 26)

Lethal - Deadly. Hagrid adores *monstrous* creatures — the more lethal, the better. (GF, Ch. 13)

Lethargy - A state of lack of energy or complete disinterest. While shut up in his room on Privet Drive, Harry *alternately* felt restless and filled with lethargy. (OP, Ch. 3)

Levitating - Floating in air. Honeydukes sells levitating sherbet balls. (PA, Ch. 10)

Liability - Something undesirable that lessens quality or introduces risk. Bertha Jorkins was gossipy and was probably viewed as a liability at the Ministry of Magic. (GF, Ch. 27)

Liberal - Abundant, providing a large amount. Hermione puts a liberal amount of jam on her toast. (GF, Ch. 13)

Linger - Hang around. Dumbledore asks Mr. Dursley to invite him in, as it is not good to linger on doorsteps. (HBP, Ch. 3)

Listlessly - Without energy. Harry gives the password to the Fat Lady after he is denied a chance to visit Hogsmeade. (PA, Ch. 8)

Livid - Very angry. After being set free Dobby attacks Lucius Malfoy, who looks livid. (CS, Ch. 18)

Loathed - Hated. Quirrell says that Harry's father and Severus Snape loathed each other, but Snape never wanted Harry dead. (SS, Ch. 17) Hermione loathed being outperformed in every potions class by Harry, whom she thought couldn't have done it without the Half-Blood Prince. (HBP, Ch. 18) Snape loathed Harry the same way he loathed Harry's father. (GF, Ch. 26)

Loathing - Hatred. Kreacher gave Sirius a look that was *redolent* of the deepest loathing. (OP, Ch. 6) At the Yule Ball, girls who had been following Viktor Krum around stared at Hermione with looks of deepest loathing. (GF, Ch. 23) Before he follows Harry's order to go work in Hogwarts' kitchens, Kreacher gives Harry a look filled with loathing. (HBP, Ch. 3)

Loftily - With a superior attitude. Percy speaks loftily. (PA, Ch. 4) Zachiarias Smith, a Hufflepuff Quidditch player, loftily makes a comment about whether or not a certain Gryffindor players has the physical body type of a beater. (HBP, Ch. 14)

Lolling - Drooping, hanging loosely. Snape's lolling head bumps on the ceiling of a tunnel as his body is *levitating*. (PA, Ch. 20)

Lolloping - Moving with a bobbing motion. As a black dog, Sirius Black is seen lolloping among with Harry and the Weasleys on the way to Kings Cross. (OP, Ch. 10)

Loon - Crazy person. In the portrait hole, Sir Cadogan calls Neville a loon because he doesn't know the password. (PA, Ch.12)

Loping - Moving with a large, natural step. The Prime Minister sees that Rufus Scrimgeour has a *rangy*, loping grace. (HBP, Ch. 1)

Ludicrous - Ridiculous. Prof. Binns says the legend of the Chamber of Secrets is a *"sensational,* even ludicrous tale." (CS, Ch. 9) Fred and George thought the idea that Harry was Slytherin's *heir* was ludicrous. (CS, Ch. 12) Hermione thinks it ludicrous to keep the Marauder's Map rather than turn it in to a teacher. (PA, Ch. 10)

Lumbago - A condition of having lower back pain. Mr. Weasley borrowed tents for the Quidditch World Cup from a friend at work who no longer camps due to lumbago. (GF, Ch. 7)

Lumbering - Moving with a heavy step. After his father tells him to go in the house, Morfin lumbers away. (HBP, Ch. 10)

Luminous - Glowing. Harry has a luminous alarm clock on Privet Drive. (PA, Ch. 1)

Lunged - Moved quickly to grab or hit someone. Lucius Malfoy lunges at Harry after Harry tricks him into freeing Dobby. (CS, Ch. 18)

Lurgy - In England, a humorous term for an illness that is not serious. When announcing a Quidditch match, Luna Lovegood says she thinks that a Hufflepuff player may be suffering from "loser's lurgy," which amused Ron greatly as he listened from his bed in the hospital wing. (HBP, Ch. 19)

Macho - Manly. Ginny spreads a rumor that Harry has Hungarian Horntail rather than hippogriff tattooed across his chest, because it's "more macho." (HBP, Ch. 25)

Maddening - Irritating. "'Well, isn't it obvious,' Hermione said with a tone of maddening superiority." (PA, Ch. 11)

Magnitude - Size. After Harry comments that Voldemort's Horcruxes could be anywhere, Dumbledore says he is glad that Harry understands the magnitude of the problem. (HBP, Ch. 23)

Maimed - Injured and disfigured. Dumbledore says that without his Horcruxes, Voldemort will be "a *mortal* man with a maimed and *diminished* soul." (HBP, Ch. 23)

Maladies - Illnesses. Katie Bell is taken to St. Mungo's Hospital for Magical Maladies and Illnesses. (HBP, Ch. 13)

Malevolent - Mean-spirited. When Malfoy finds Ron alone at the Shrieking Shack, his face "split in a malevolent grin." (PA, Ch. 14) When Filch suspects that Peeves stole an egg from a Triwizard champion, he whispers to Snape about it malevolently. (GF, Ch. 25)

Malfunctioning - Not working correctly. Ron's broken wand is malfunctioning. (CS, Ch. 7)

Malice - Spite, evil intent. With malice, Snape tells Karkaroff that Harry has a habit of breaking rules. (GF, Ch. 17)

Maliciously - With a desire to harm. Harry thinks Malfoy's eyes glint maliciously. (PA, Ch. 5, 6)

Mallet - A fat hammer made or wood or rubber, used to pound objects such as tent stakes. Mr. Weasley gets overexcited about using a mallet when putting up tents in the Quidditch World Cup. (GF, Ch. 7)

Manacle - Handcuff. Peter Pettigrew turns back into a rat to escape his manacle. (PA, Ch. 20)

Mane - Large amount of hair. Mad-Eye Moody has a long mane of *grizzled* hair. (GF, Ch. 14)

Mangy - Shabby. Sir Cadogan calls Harry a "mangy *cur*." (PA, Ch. 9)

Manhandle - Grab or push aggressively. After Dolores Umbridge grabs and shakes Marietta Edgecombe, Dumbledore casts a spell that makes her hands burn and says, "I cannot allow you to manhandle my students, Dolores." (OP, Ch. 27)

Mania - Crazy enthusiasm. Harry is shocked that Hermione didn't do something to stop Romilda Vane from pursuing her plan to slip him a love potion, especially in light of Hermione's mania for upholding rules. (HBP, Ch. 15)

Maniac - A crazy, possibly violent person. Ginny Weasley *blanched* when Ron said he hoped the maniac terrorizing Hogwarts would petrify Filch before he's caught. (CS, Ch. 9)

Manic - Wildly energetic, to the point of being insane. Oliver Wood regains his manic energy after a loss to Hufflepuff in Quidditch. (PA, Ch. 10) Uncle Vernon smiles a manic grin as he tells neighbors that the loud bang they just heard must have been a car backfiring. (OP, Ch. 1)

Manifest - Show. Hermione gives Harry a funny look as if strange *symptoms* might manifest at any moment. (HBP, Ch. 5)

Manky - In England, rotten or falling apart. The Portkey that Harry uses to go to Hogwarts is a manky old boot. (GF, Ch. 6)

Mannish - Like a man (used to refer to a woman or child). Rita Skeeter has large, mannish hands. (GF, Ch. 18)

Marauder - A pirate or other criminal who searches a territory for things to steal. The Marauder's Map looks like an old bit of parchment until one speaks the proper words to make it reveal itself. (PA, Ch. 10)

Marginally - To a small degree. After a disastrous Quidditch practice, Harry notices that Ron looks marginally more cheerful after a bit of conversation. (HBP, Ch. 14)

Marshal - Organize. Voldemort uses Fenrir Greyback to marshal the werewolves. (HBP, Ch. 16)

Masquerading - Pretending. The Minister of Magic urges wizards to develop security questions to ask each other to *ensure* that they are not fooled by dark wizards using Polyjuice Potion to masquerade as someone else. (HBP, Ch. 3)

Mass - Pertaining to a large group or a huge amount. Giants were involved in mass killings of Muggles. (GF Ch. 24) Harry finds the lake at Hogwarts to be an iron-gray mass of chilly water. (GF, Ch. 26)

Massive - Huge. Harry tells Stan Shunpike he saw something like a dog, but massive. (PA, Ch. 3)

Materialized - Appeared seemingly out of nowhere. Mundungus Fletcher materialized after Harry battled with the dementors. (OP, Ch. 2)

Maternal - Motherly. Hagrid tells Madame Maxine that his mother wasn't really "the maternal sort." (GF, Ch. 23)

Mayhem - Disorder. Hermione says Ron and Harry need to create some mayhem so she can steal items for the Polyjuice Potion from Snape's storeroom. (CS, Ch. 11)

Meddle - Get involved with something that is none of one's business. Dobby warns Harry that he must not meddle with the Chamber of Secrets because it's too dangerous. (CS, Ch. 10)

Medieval - Old, fearful, superstitious. The Dursley have a "medieval attitude" about wizardry. (PA, Ch. 1)

Melodramatic - Overly dramatic. Harry thought Voldemort arranged for him to become a Triwizard champion to arrange his death in the competition, but didn't tell Ron so because it would have sounded melodramatic. (GF, Ch. 17)

Menace - A bully or stalker; also the quality of being threatening. Peeves is described as "a grinning, airborne menace who lived to cause havoc and distress." (CS, Ch. 8) Moody speaks to Snape with a voice that is full of menace. (GF, Ch. 25)

Menacing - Threatening. *Surly* security trolls pace the corridor in a menacing group, talking in grunts and comparing the size of their clubs." (PA, Ch. 14)

Menacingly - In a threatening manner. Snape's eyes flash menacingly at the mention of Prof. Lupin. (PA, Ch. 8)

Mere - By itself. Snape's mere presence is usually enough to *ensure* that a class is quiet. (OP, Ch. 12)

Mesmerized - Fascinated, as if held in a spell. Harry is surrounded by mesmerized girls on the Hogwarts Express. (HBP, Ch. 7)

Midges - A tiny, two-winged fly. Ludo Bagman waves away Barty Crouch's warning about announcing plans for the Tri-Wizard Cup as if his objections were midges. (GF, Ch. 7)

Mimic - Imitate. Hermione puts a charm on coins so that if Harry changes the numbers on his coin, all the other coins will mimic his. (OP, Ch. 19)

Miming - Portraying something without words. Harry sees Draco miming the shattering of a nose, presumably Harry's. (HBP, Ch. 8)

Mingled - Mixed together. Harry delivers a flask of a potion he brewed to Prof. Snape with mingled feelings of *defiance* and relief. (OP, Ch. 15) Ron's face shows mingled surprise and *exasperation* when Harry orders Dobby and Kreacher to follow Draco. (HBP, Ch. 19)

Minions - Lowly assistants of a powerful person. Malfoy and Bulstrode are Umbridge's minions. (OP, Ch. 32)

Miniscule - Tiny. The names of people appear in miniscule writing next to tiny dots that move on the Marauder's Map. (PA, Ch. 10) Out of a purple silk sack, Harry pulled a miniature Hungarian Horntail dragon with miniscule fangs. (GF, Ch. 20)

Ministrations - Acts of aid. Ron leaves the hospital wing after being poisoned, thanks to Harry's quick thinking and the ministrations of Madam Pomfrey. (HBP, Ch. 20)

Mirthless - Without happiness. Voldemort has a mirthless laugh. (GF, Ch. 1)

Miscarriage - Bad management. Dumbledore says the Wizengamot must hear testimony from a witness more than once if the alternative is a miscarriage of justice. (OP, Ch. 8)

Miscreants - Criminals or other rule-breaking people. Filch loves nothing more than catching a miscreant. (OP, Ch. 30)

Misfortune - Bad luck. Mr. Weasley suggests that Winky simply had the misfortune of picking up Harry's wand after someone else used it to *conjure* the Dark Mark. (GF, Ch. 9)

Misguided - Doing the wrong thing while thinking it's the right thing. Percy says his parents are misguided in their loyalty to Dumbledore. (OP, Ch. 14)

Misshapen - Oddly formed. Hermione's hats for house elves look to Harry like misshapen woolen objects. (OP, Ch. 13)

Missive - Letter. Harry keeps rereading the missive he received from Dumbledore in which he said he would take Harry from Privet Drive to The Burrow. (HBP, Ch. 3)

Mobilize - Move into action. Ministry of Magic officials fear that Dumbledore might raise an army that he could mobilize against the Ministry. (OP, Ch. 16)

Modifications - Changes. The Prime Minister hears Cornelius Fudge tell him that he should not worry about Muggle witnesses to events at the "Kwidditch" World Cup because those individuals have had "memory modifications." (HBP, Ch. 1)

Modified - Changed. When Harry sees a look of dreamy unconcern on the face of Mr. Roberts, a Muggle working at the site of the Quidditch World Cup, he realizes that the man just had his memory modified. (GF, Ch. 7)

Moldering - Decaying, turning to dust. If a Muggle came upon Hogwarts, he or she would just see a moldering old ruin, according to Hermione. (GF, Ch. 10)

Mollified - Made to feel less upset. Hermione looks mollified after Ron tells her that she's cleverer than Harry and himself. (OP, Ch. 12)

Momentarily - Temporarily. After the Quidditch World Cup, a flash of green light momentarily lit up the campsite. (GF, Ch. 9)

Monocle - A kind of eyeglass with just one lens. A witch at Harry's hearing in the Ministry of Magic wears a monocle. (OP, Ch. 8)

Monotonous - Boring, unchanging. Prof. Binns lectures in a monotonous *drone*. (OP, Ch. 17)

Monotony - The same thing, over and over; boredom. Sirius says he doesn't know why Harry is complaining about the visit of the dementors to Little Whinging, because it seems to him they broke up the monotony rather nicely. (OP, Ch. 5)

Monstrous - Huge. Harry sees that the Hungarian Horntail is a monstrous lizard. (GF, Ch. 20)

Moor - A tract of land not much good for farming. The Sorting Hat sings that Gyffindor grew up in a moor, Ravenclaw in a *glen,* Hufflepuff in a valley and Slytherin in a *fen.* (GF, Ch. 12)

Moored - Tied to a fixed place, such as a dock or anchor. The Durmstrang ship is moored in the lake on Hogwarts' grounds. (GF, Ch. 24)

Morale - Spirit, dedication to an endeavor. Ron has a tough time maintaining his morale in Quidditch. (OP, Ch. 19) Fudge admits that morale at the Ministry of Magic is low after the murder of Amelia Bones. (HBP, Ch. 1) When Dumbledore says Harry's powers won't "register compared to mine" in a boat meant for one wizard, it doesn't raise Harry's morale. (HBP, Ch. 26)

Morosely - Gloomily. Moaning Myrtle gurgles morosely in one of the toilets while Harry waits for the Polyjuice Potion to take effect. (CS, Ch. 12) Fudge looks morosely at the "Minister of Muggles" as they discuss the Bones and Vance murders and other terrible events. (HBP, Ch. 1) Hagrid recalls morosely that he raised Aragog from when he was just an egg. (HBP, Ch. 22)

Mortal - Destined to die; human. Dumbledore says that without his Horcruxes, Voldemort will be "a mortal man with a *maimed* and *diminished* soul." (HBP, Ch. 23)

Mortality rate - Deaths per year. Slughorn tells Harry he does not want to teach at Hogwarts because he does not like the mortality rate among professors. (HBP, Ch. 4)

Mortified - Very embarrassed. Ron stopped craning his neck and looked mortified when Neville's grandmother explained why Neville's parents were in St. Mungo's. (OP, Ch. 23) Molly Weasley is mortified when she proves she is not a Death Eater to her husband by revealing her nickname: Mollywobbles. (HBP, Ch. 5)

Mournfully - Sadly. The "Minister of Muggles" looks around his office mournfully. (HBP, Ch.1)

Mullioned - Divided up the middle. Many windows in the Harry Potter books are described as mullioned.

Mundane - Ordinary, commonplace. "Allow your eyes to see past the mundane!" Prof. Trelawney urges her students. (PA, Ch. 6)

Mutating - Changing form. Snape describes fighting a dark wizard as battling something that unfixed and mutating. (HBP, Ch. 9)

Mutilated - Badly damaged and disfigured. Mad-Eye Moody has a mutilated face. (GF, Ch. 16) Dumbledore tells Harry that when Voldemort discovered that Tom Riddle's diary had been mutilated, he was enraged. (HBP, Ch. 23)

Mutinous - Challenging those in charge. When Prof. McGonagall announces that testing will continue despite attacks that have petrified students, there is mutinous muttering among her students. (PA, Ch. 16) When the referee at the Quidditch World Cup demands the veela stop dancing, they look mutinous. (GF, Ch. 8) Fred and George have mutinous expressions when Dumbledore says he will make sure that no Hogwarts student under the age of 17 tricks an impartial judge into selecting him or her as Hogwarts champion in the Triwizard Tournament. (GF, Ch. 12) Dean Thomas *stoically* took the news that he was being benched in Quidditch, but Harry worried that he and Seamus were muttering mutinously behind his back. (HBP, Ch. 24)

Nancy - An insulting term used to describe a boy who's girlish. After Dudley got bad marks in school, Uncle Vernon brushed it off, saying, he didn't want "some *swotty* little nancy boy for a son anyway." (GF, Ch. 3)

Naive (pronounced "NIGH-eve") - An insulting term for not recognizing what's really going on or is about to happen. Hermione says Harry is naive for thinking Umbridge won't blame Hagrid for putting a niffler in her office, even without proof. (OP, Ch. 31)

Naught - Zero or nothing. The sphinx in the Tri-Wizard Cup competition gives Harry a riddle that includes the line, "Think first of the person who lives in disguise/Who deals in secrets and tells naught but lies." (GF, Ch. 31)

Neglecting - Ignoring someone or something for which one is responsible. Dumbledore accuses the Dursleys of neglecting Harry. (HBP, Ch. 3)

Niceties - Polite habits. Voldemort demands Harry bow before dueling, saying that the niceties must be observed. (GF, Ch. 34)

Niche (pronounced "nitch" or "neesh") - A place for something or a market for a particular product. Barty Crouch knows a businessman who is convinced that there is a niche for flying carpets in wizard shops because they can be used to transport a whole family. (GF, Ch. 7)

Nicked - In England, robbed. Harry doesn't want to turn in the Marauder's Map because he would have to explain that he got it from Fred and George, who nicked it from Filch's office. (PA, Ch. 10)

Noble - Doing the right thing, even at one's own expense or risk. Dobby calls Harry, "So noble! So *valiant!*" (CS, Ch. 10)

Nonchalantly - Casually. A pony grazes in a field in a painting nonchalantly (PA, Ch. 6).

Noncommittal - Neutral, not committing to anything. Harry made noncommittal noises when Hermione asked probing questions about what grade he received in potions. (OP, Ch. 15) Harry made a noncommittal gesture when Molly Weasley asked him if he liked Slughorn after he met him for the first time. (HBP, Ch. 4)

Nonentity - Object or person that does not exist, a nobody. Malfoy observes that *The Daily Prophet* gets Arthur Weasley's name wrong and concludes, "It's almost as if he's a complete nonentity, isn't it?" (GF, Ch. 13)

Nonplussed - Confused or perplexed. Ron is *utterly* nonplused when Luna Lovegood is bowled over with laughter at a remark that Ron considered amusing but not exactly *hysterical*. (OP, Ch. 10) Harry is nonplussed after he falls into the pensieve and finds that no one can hear him or see him. (GF, Ch. 30)

Notorious - Famous for something negative. Dumbledore says Tom Riddle's desire was to not be ordinary but be perceived as different, separate and notorious. (HBP, Ch. 13)

Notoriously - Having to do with being known for something bad. Rita Skeeter writes that Alastor "Mad-Eye" Moody has a reputation for being "notoriously jinx-happy" because he has a habit of attacking anyone who makes a sudden movement in his presence." (GF, Ch. 24)

Notwithstanding - Despite. Dumbledore promises Slughorn that he will be welcome to visit Hogwarts notwithstanding its increased security precautions. (HBP, Ch. 4)

Noxious - Poisonous. Sirius's gloomy mood seem to seep through 12 Grimmauld Place like some noxious gas. (OP, Ch. 24)

Nutter - In England, an insulting term for a crazy person. Mad-Eye Moody has a reputation as a nutter, according to George Weasley. (GF, Ch. 10) Ron says he thinks Sirius Black and Lupin are both nutters until they tell him the truth about Scabbers. (PA, Ch. 18)

Objective (adjective) - Based on facts and reason, not opinion. Lucius Malfoy tells *The Daily Prophet* that Dolores Umbridge's appointment as Hogwarts High Inquisitor is a good thing because she will be able to provide an objective evaluation of Dumbledore. (OP, Ch. 15)

Obliging - Helpful, cooperative. An owl held out an obliging leg for Cho Chang to attach a parcel. (OP, Ch. 14)

Oblivious - Not noticing or paying attention. Hermione acts oblivious to the tension between Ron and Lavender, but Harry notices an *inexplicable* smirk on her face. (HBP, Ch. 20)

Obscure (adjective) - Out of the way, not well-known. Occlumency is an obscure branch of magic. (OP, Ch. 24)

Obscure (verb) - To make dark, hidden or hard to see. Harry and Cedric see a Death Eater with a hood that obscures his face. (GF, Ch. 32)

Obscured - Hidden. Harry's vision is suddenly obscured by a large amount of bushy hair as Hermione hugs him. (OP, Ch. 4) The windows of the Hogwarts Express become obscured with steam just before Tonks hustles Harry off. (HBP, Ch. 8)

Obsessed - Thinking of nothing else. Lord Voldemort tells Wormtail that the Ministry can be expected to be obsessed with security at the Quidditch World Cup. (GF, Ch. 1)

Obsessively - Excessively, as if one is obsessed. Aunt Petunia obsessively follows news about a celebrity divorce even though she pretends not to be interested in such *sordid* affairs. (OP, Ch. 1)

Obsolete - Out of date. Rita Skeeter reminds Dumbledore about an article she wrote in which she described him as an obsolete dingbat. (GF, Ch. 18)

Obstinate - Stubborn and hard-headed. Asked if he had been reading Rita Skeeter, Fudge is obstinate and defiant. (GF, Ch. 36)

Obstructed - Blocked. Alicia Spinnet's vision is obstructed after a curse makes her eyebrows grow. (OP, Ch. 19) The Impediment Curse can slow down and obstruct attackers. (GF, Ch. 31)

Obstruction - Blockage. Harry feels a slight obstruction in his chest when Ron and Hermione act supportive of him, rather than pull away in fear, when they learn that Dumbledore is going to train Harry to fight Voldemort. (HBP, Ch. 5)

Oddment - One of a group of items that together might be called odds and ends. Dumbledore gives a speech of "a few words," specifically: "Nitwit! Blubber! Oddment! Tweak!" (SS, Ch. 7)

Offensive - Rude. Dean Thomas realizes that he said something very offensive to Firenze when he asked whether Hagrid had bred centaurs. (OP, Ch. 27)

Omen - Sign of something that will happen. Prof. Trelawney says the Grim is an omen of death. (PA, Ch. 6)

Ominous - Scary and hinting about things to come. Harry thinks it is ominous that Hagrid thought he needed a biting book. (PA, Ch. 1) When Hagrid stops coming to the castle for meals, Harry takes it as an ominous sign. (HBP, Ch. 11)

Omniscient - All-knowing. When Dumbledore surprised Voldemort by naming his traveling companions, Voldemort says, "You are as omniscient as ever, Dumbledore." (HBP, Ch. 20)

Opaline - Like opal, a glittering stone. The sky was opaline in winter at Hogwarts. (PA, Ch. 10)

Opaque - Unable to be seen through. A window is opaque with hammering rain while Hermione wonders if starting the DA was the right thing to do. (OP, Ch. 18) In the middle of the lake, the water became opaque. (GF, Ch. 26)

Oppression - Keeping someone or something down. Hermione says wizards are *colluding* in the oppression of house elves. (GF, Ch. 15)

Orb - A round, ball-like object. When Lupin confronts the boggart, it turns into a white orb. (PA, Ch. 11)

Ornate - Fancy. At 12 Grimmauld Place, Harry sees an ornate bottle filled with what he's certain is blood. (OP, Ch. 6)

Otherworldly - Strange, as if from another planet. When merpeople sing at Dumbledore's funeral, the sound is otherworldly. (HBP, Ch. 30)

Outcast - A person who is shunned by a group to which he or she formerly belonged. Dumbledore says he cannot ask Firenze to return to the forest because he is now an outcast among his kind. (HBP, Ch. 20)

Outrage - Extreme disapproval. Bellatrix LeStrange's voice is full of outrage when Snape tells her that he responded to Voldemort's call for Death Eaters through the Dark Mark only after Dumbledore told him to, but her outrage cools when Snape points out this was necessary to remain at Hogwarts as a spy. (HBP, Ch. 2)

Overblown - Too big, out of proportion. Ludo Bagman looked like a slightly overblown cartoon figure among the Triwizard champions. (GF, Ch. 20)

Overexert - Expend too much energy, to the point of making oneself ill. Madam Pomfrey says Harry will recover from his cracked skull but that he should not overexert himself. When Harry says he wants to leave to find McClaggan and kill him, Madam Pomfrey says, "I'm afraid that would come under the heating of 'overexertion.'" (HBP, Ch. 19)

Overindulged - Ate or drank to excess. After Christmas, the password to enter the Gryffindor Common Room is *"abstinence,"* and Hermione explains that the Fat Lady and a friend overindulged by drinking all the wine in a picture in the Charms corridor. (HBP, Ch. 17)

Overstatement - Exaggeration. When Cornelius Fudge tells the Prime Minister that different groups in the wizarding world are at war, the Prime Minister optimistically asks if the description is an overstatement. (HBP, Ch. 1)

Overt - Obvious. Harry notices that Snape seems *wary* of displaying overt *animosity* to Mad-Eye Moody. (GF, Ch. 14)

Overwrought - Stressed out. Harry's overwrought brain dreams about exams every night. (OP, Ch. 30)

Pacify - Calm. Ron throws some owl treats to Hedwig and Pigwidgeon to pacify them. (OP, Ch. 6)

Packing case - In England, a large, strong box. Lupin heaves a packing case containing a boggart onto a desk so Harry can practice conjuring a Patronus. (PA, Ch. 11)

Paddock - An enclosure in which animals can walk around and graze. In Hagrid's first Care of Magical Creatures class, students see a dozen hippogriffs in a paddock. (PA, Ch. 6)

Palpable - Able to be felt with one's skin. Before the Quidditch World Cup, excitement rose like a palpable cloud over the campsite. (GF, Ch. 7)

Panicky - Nervous. Hermione is panicky when she thinks Harry wants to murder Sirius Black in an act of revenge. (PA, Ch. 11) Harry is panicky when Dumbledore shows up at Privet Drive. (HBP, Ch. 3)

Paranoid - Overly fearful and suspicious. Ron says Mad-Eye Moody is paranoid. (GF, Ch. 15)

Parched - Dry, thirsty. At the beginning of Book Five, the lawns on Privet Drive are parched and yellowing due to hot weather. (OP, Ch. 1)

Parchment - Old-style paper. Hogwarts students receive assignments to write essays on parchment, and the Marauder's Map appears like an old bit of parchment until the proper words make it reveal itself. (PA, Ch. 10)

Parentage - Ancestry. "Mudblood" is an insulting term referring to people of Muggle parentage. (GF, Ch. 9)

Partisan - Loyal to one side. Snape shows he is partisan to Slytherin's Quidditch team by booking the pitch so often that Gryffindors have difficulty getting on it to practice. (OP, Ch. 19)

Passable - Barely acceptable. Slughorn declares that Malfoy's Hiccupping Solution is merely passable. (HBP, Ch. 22)

Pate - Scalp. Because he is bald, Horace Slughorn has a shiny pate. (HBP, Ch. 4)

Paternally - Like a father. Gilderoy Lockhart paternally gives advice to Harry about handling fame. (CS, Ch. 6)

Patronizing - Acting as if someone is inferior. Fleur Delacour gives Harry a patronizing look. (GF, Ch. 18)

Pathetic - Disgustingly sad. Malfoy calls Hagrid pathetic as he cries for Buckbeak, who has been sentenced to death. (PA, Ch. 15)

Paunchy - Chubby. The photographer for *The Daily Prophet* who accompanies Rita Skeeter is described as paunchy. (GF, Ch. 18)

Peaceable - Quietly behaved, peaceful. Dumbledore tells Harry that once they take the Horcrux, he expects the Inferi guarding it to be less peaceable. (HBP, Ch. 26)

Peaky - In England, looking pale and unhealthy. When Harry arrives at 12 Grimmauld Place, Mrs. Weasley fusses over him and says he looks peaky. (OP, Ch. 4)

Peckish - In England, slightly hungry. Fred Weasley says house elves love being helpful and that if you tell one that you're feeling peckish, he'll bring you a roast ox. (GF, Ch. 21)

Pending - Temporary, awaiting a future event or decision. Harry receives a polite message from the Ministry of Magic telling him he should consider himself suspended from Hogwarts "pending further inquiries." (OP, Ch. 2)

Pensively - Quietly lost in though. Hermione speaks pensively when Harry asks her why Snape hates Lupin so much. (PA, Ch. 9)

Perchance - Perhaps. Sir Cadogan wonders if Harry, Ron and Hermione are staring at his painting because they are amused that he has fallen off his horse: "Come to *scorn* at my fall, perchance?" (PA, Ch. 5)

Perimeter - Outside edge. Harry followed Hagrid around the perimeter of the forest and came upon dragons. (GF, Ch. 19)

Perish - Die. Sir Cadogan pledges he will help Harry, Ron and Hermione find the North Tower or "perish bravely in the charge!" (PA, Ch. 5)

Permeate - Soak through. When Mrs. Weasley is yelling at Mundungus Fletcher for bringing stolen goods into the Order of the Phoenix's hideout, Fred opens the door to allow the sound of her voice to permeate the room. (OP, Ch. 6) At the Three Broomsticks, the grime on the windows is so thick that little daylight can permeate it. (OP, Ch. 16)

Perpetrator - Person who commits a crime. Molly Weasley says that after Voldemort's return, some wizards sold worthless defensive potions and that the perpetrators were crooks like Mundungus Fletcher. (HBP, Ch. 5)

Persistent - Trying repeatedly. Glasses that Dumbledore conjures are persistent in knocking themselves against the Dursleys' heads. (HBP, Ch. 3)

Perturbed - Annoyed. Ludo Bagman looks perturbed when Viktor Krum asks to speak to Harry. (GF, Ch. 28)

Perusing - Looking over. Uncle Vernon is perusing a letter from Mrs. Weasley when he comes across a word he considers quite strange: Quidditch. (GF, Ch. 3) Harry pretends to perusing a book on venoms to avoid talking about the possibility of his teaching others about fighting dark wizards. (OP, Ch. 16)

Pestilential - Irritating; full of something that is harmful or life-threatening. Uncle Vernon doesn't believe Harry is interested in the Muggle news, saying, "As if we didn't know that you get all your news from those pestilential birds!" (OP, Ch. 1) Before he agrees to return to Hogwarts, Slughorn tells Dumbledore he would never go back to that pestilential school. (HBP, Ch. 4)

Petrol - In England, gasoline. Bobotuber pus smells like petrol. (GF, Ch. 13)

Petty - Unimportant or small-minded. Rita Skeeter reports that Hagrid considers himself above the government's petty rules on breeding new forms of magical creatures. (GF, Ch. 24)

Pewter - A type of metal. Hagrid drinks from a pewter tankard. (PA, Ch. 6)

Phenomenal - Unbelievably good. Harry and Ron talk about the Firebolt, including its phenomenal acceleration. (PA, Ch. 13)

Phlegm - Mucus. Ginny's nickname for Fleur is Phlegm. (HBP, Ch. 5)

Physique - The shape of one's body. After dieting and learning to box, Dudley remained a very large boy but with a more muscular physique. (OP, Ch. 1)

Pilfering - Stealing. After Harry drops his egg on a staircase, Flich assumes it was dropped by Peeves, and he calls out for the "pilfering *poltergeist*." (GF, Ch. 25)

Pillock - In England, an offensive term for silly person. Bill Weasley says Rita Skeeter once wrote that he was a "long-haired pillock" in a story about Gringott's charm breakers. (GF, Ch. 10)

Pinched - Thin and pale. After a summer on Privet Drive, and a growth spurt, Harry had a pinched, slightly unhealthy look. (OP, Ch. 1)

Pining - Desperately desiring. Winky is pining to return home to Mr. Crouch. (GF, Ch. 28)

Pinioned - Restrained by the arms. Harry sees Hermione pinioned by Millicent Bulstrode. (OP, Ch. 32)

Pirouette - A spin in place. Crabbe did a pirouette in midair at the Shrieking Shack after Harry, hidden by his invisibility cloak, threw a stick at his back. (PA, Ch. 14) Hermione did a graceful pirouette while practicing to apparate. (HBP, Ch. 22)

Pitch - In England, an athletic field. Wood, unable to come up with a pre-game speech, just *beckons* to the Gryffindor team to follow him to the Quidditch pitch. (PA, Ch. 9)

Pitiable - Deserving of either pity or a mixture of pity and scorn (because the person or thing is so inadequate). Snape says that while Voldemort was living in Quirrel's body, he was in a pitiable condition, "very weak" and "sharing the body of a mediocre wizard." (HBP, Ch. 2)

Pittance - Tiny amount of money. Hepzibah correctly guesses that Borgin only paid a pittance for Slytherin's locket. (HBP, Ch. 20)

Placatingly - Soothingly. Sirius speaks placatingly to Harry, who is upset at what he saw his father do in Snape's pensieve. (OP, Ch. 29)

Placidly - Calmly, serenely. After having his memory modified, a Muggle rental agent placidly hands a map to Mr. Weasley. (GF, Ch. 7) When Dumbledore hands a blank piece of paper to Mrs. Cole at Tom Riddle's orphanage, she looks at it and says placidly, "That seems perfectly in order." (HBP, Ch. 13) When Harry discovers that Inferi are in the water surrounding a Horcrux, Dumbledore says placidly that they do not have to worry about them for the moment. (HBP, Ch. 26)

Plaintively — In a way suggesting hidden sadness. Filch plaintively explains to Snape that he must continue pursuing Peeves because he thinks this will be his opportunity to get rid of the *poltergeist* once and for all. (GF, Ch. 25) Moaning Myrtle says plaintively about Draco Malfoy, "I thought he liked me." (HBP, Ch. 21) Slughorn sings plaintively in Hagrid's hut just before Harry decides to press him for the memory of Tom Riddle that Dumbledore wants. (HBP, Ch. 22)

Plotting - Planning. Frank Bryce overheads Voldemort and Wormtail plotting a murder. (GF, Ch. 1)

Ploy - Tricky strategic move. While watching the Quidditch World Cup, Harry sees an Irish player make a darting move called Porskoff Ploy. (GF, Ch. 8)

Plummeted - Sank. Harry's heart plummeted as he wondered if Hermione had told Prof. McGonagall that he had gone to Hogsmeade without permission. (PA, Ch. 14)

Podium - Small wooden stand, usually used by public speakers. Harry sees the Firebolt sitting on a podium at Quality Quidditch Supplies. (PA, Ch. 4)

Poltergeist - Ghost or spirit that haunts a place. After Harry drops his egg on a staircase, Flich assumes it was dropped by Peeves, and he calls out for the "*pilfering* poltergeist." (GF, Ch. 25) Snape says he doesn't "give a damn" about Peeves, "that *wretched* poltergeist." (GF, Ch. 25)

Pompous - Thinking oneself or what one has to say to be very important. Percy follows Harry around like a "pompous guard dog" after Sirius Black has been spotted inside Gryffindor Tower. (PA, Ch. 9) Percy greets and shakes hands with Harry pompously, as if Percy were the mayor. (PA, Ch. 4) Harry likes Ernie Macmillan despite his pompous manner. (HBP, Ch. 9)

Popinjay - A proud person who acts superior. After Harry angrily complains that no one is telling him anything, Phineas Nigellus calls him a puffed-up popinjay. (OP, Ch. 23)

Portent - Omen or sign of things to come. Prof. Trelawnly babbles about "certain dark portents I have glimpsed" and "omens I have been *vouchsafed*" before Harry gets her attention by asking whether she had been trying to enter the Room of Requirement. (HBP, Ch. 25)

Portentously - Pompously. Ernie Macmillan speaks portentously. (HBP, Ch. 9)

Possessions - Things that belong to a person. Dumbledore tells Harry, "you *inherit* all of Sirius' possessions." (HBP, Ch. 3)

Pottering - Puttering; wandering aimlessly or working in a disorganized way. At age 77, Frank Bryce, a Riddle family employee, could still be seen pottering around the flower beds. (GF, Ch. 1)

Pouf - A cushiony footstool or a couch with no back, also called an ottoman. In Sibyll Trelawney's divination class, students sit on poufs (PA, Ch. 6).

Prat -In England, a jerk. When Neville voices the opinion that Harry will have to fight the Cruciatus Curse in the Triwizard Tournament, George Weasley points out the curse is illegal and says, "Don't be a prat, Neville." (GF, Ch. 21) Pansy Parkinson says a Ravenclaw named Belby is a prat. (HBP, Ch. 7) Fred says his brother Percy may be the world's biggest prat. (HBP, Ch 16)

Preamble - Introductory remarks. Without any form of greeting or preamble, Harry asks Moody whether he was able to locate Mr. Crouch. (GF, Ch. 29)

Precariously - Delicately balanced. Rita Skeeter perches herself precariously on an upturned bucket when she interviews Harry at the Triwizard Tournament. (GF, Ch. 18) A hat shaped like a lion's head was precariously perched on Luna Lovegood's head. (OP, Ch. 19)

Precautionary - Protective. Lupin keeps a precautionary hand on Harry's arm to make sure he doesn't plunge into an archway into which Sirius disappeared at the Department of Mysteries. (OP, Ch. 36)

Precautions - Steps taken to prevent something from happening. Snape reminds Cornelius Fudge of all the precautions that Hogwarts had taken to prevent Harry from being attacked, yet he *consorted* with "a werewolf and a murderer." (PA, Ch. 20) Dumbledore asks Slughorn about the precautions he has taken to hide himself. (HBP, Ch. 4)

Preceded - Came before. Wizards can tell what spells came out of a wand - the most recent spell first, followed by those that preceded it. (GF, Ch. 36)

Predecessor - Person who had the job or role before. Cornelius Fudge tells the Prime Minister that he reacted to Fudge's visit much better than his predecessor, who assume Fudge was a hoax. (HBP, Ch. 1)

Predisposed - Likely to take a certain action due to opinions previously formed. The Ministry of Magic was predisposed to suspect Hokey because wizards tended to view house elves as inferior beings. (HBP, Ch. 20)

Preened - Brushed one's hair or smoothed one's clothes. At the Quidditch World Cup you could buy figurines of players who moved around and preened. (GF, Ch. 7)

Preferential - Specially cared for. McLaggen thought he might get preferential treatment from Harry in Quidditch tryouts because they were both among Slughorn's favorites. (HBP, Ch. 11)

Pregnant - Full of meaning. While everyone knows pregnant can refer to a woman who is going to have a baby, it can also refer to a moment that is full of meaning, like the pregnant pause in Ron and Harry's conversation in the Chamber of Secrets. (CS, Ch. 16)

Prejudice - Attitude of not liking anyone who is part of a certain group, often easily identified by how they look. Hermione thinks all the *hysteria* over giants is just prejudice and *bigotry*. (GF, Ch. 24) Slughorn says he was surprised at the talents of Harry's mother considering that she was Muggle-born, then adds, "You mustn't think I'm prejudiced!"

Premises - Location. Fred and George leave Hogwarts by inviting everyone to visit "our new premises" — Weasleys' Wizard Wheezes on Diagon Alley. (OP, Ch. 29) Cornelius Fudge informs the Prime Minister that Sirius Black was murdered on Ministry of Magic premises, which prompts the Prime Minister to feel a "fleeting stab of pity" for Fudge. (HBP, Ch. 1)

Premonition - Thought that could be a prediction of the future. Prof. Trelawney sees an odd look on Harry face and wonders if he has had a premonition. (GF, Ch. 29)

Preoccupation - Excessive concern with a single idea or subject. Mrs. Weasley displays preoccupation with pajamas until she understands that Ron has been made a prefect. (OP, Ch. 9)

Preposterous - Ridiculous. When told by Dumbledore that children are considered adults at the age of 17 in the wizarding world, Vernon Dursley says, "Preposterous." (HBP, Ch. 3) Fudge thinks Dumbledore's idea of removing the dementors from Azkaban is preposterous. (GF, Ch. 36)

Prestigious - Of high reputation. *The Daily Prophet* says Dumbledore's *eccentric* decisions have raised questions about whether he is still up to managing the prestigious school of wizardry. (OP, Ch. 15)

Presumably - For an assumed reason. Prof. McGonagall was absent from the Great Hall, presumably because she was supervising a clean up after Peeves' water balloon attack. (GF, Ch. 12) Cedric's face is covered with a thick orange paste, presumably to mend a dragon burn. (GF, Ch. 20)

Pretense - State of pretending something is true when its not. When the dementors show up in Little Whinging, Aunt Petunia is forced to give up the pretense that the wizarding world simply did not exist. (OP, Ch. 2) Abandoning pretense, Harry asks Lupin whether he was the Half-Blood Prince. (HBP, Ch. 16) Dumbledore asks Draco Malfoy to drop the pretense that he is a killer and abandon dark magic. (HBP, Ch. 27)

Pretext - False reason. On the pretext of moving himself closer to a table, Harry managed to get a view of the Quidditch pitch. (OP, Ch. 13) Harry sneaked a glance at Snape and Karkaroff through the pretext of holding up a measuring cup. (GF, Ch. 27)

Prise - In England, to force with a lever. Several people tried to prise the portrait of the ugly little man off the wall in the Prime Minister's office, but it could not be removed. (HBP, Ch. 1)

Problematic - Difficult, troublesome. Dumbledore tells Harry that he has inherited all of Sirius' *possessions*, but the problematic part concerns 12 Grimmauld Place. (HBP, Ch. 3)

Procedure - Way of doing things. Arthur and Molly Weasley follow a Ministry of Magic procedure to quiz each other and *ensure* the other is not an *imposter*. (HBP, Ch. 5)

Procession - One after another. When Harry arrives at Hogwarts, he sees stagecoaches led by invisible horses that bump and sway in procession (PA, Ch. 5).

Procure - Obtain. Luna Lovegood managed to procure a hat shaped like a lion's head to support Gryffindor in its Quidditch match. (OP, Ch. 19) When he learns that Hagrid is about to bury an acromantula, Slughorn wonders whether it might be possible to procure some venom from the giant spider before it is buried. (HBP, Ch. 22) Dumbledore compliments Harry on procuring an important memory from Slughorn. (HBP, Ch. 23)

Prodding - Poking. Harry sees Hermione prodding leeches as she prepares Polyjuice Potion (CS, Ch. 11)

Proffered - Offered. Harry holds Dumbledore's proffered forearm before they apparate. (HBP, Ch. 4)

Proffering - Presenting. When Harry and his friends encounter Neville's grandmother at St. Mungo's, they see that she is proffering her hand *regally*. (OP, Ch. 23)

Profoundly - Deeply, incredibly. "Which profoundly foolish person wrote down this week's passwords and left them lying around?" Prof. McGonagall asks. (It's Neville.) (PA, Ch. 13)

Progressively - In a growing or shrinking way. Fred and George bewitched a photo of Harry to issue insults about Umbridge in a booming voice, but over time the voice became progressively higher. (OP, Ch. 26)

Prolonged - Taking up a lot of time. After a prolonged snore is emitted from what Harry assumed was a pile of rages, Mundungus Fletcher is awakened by the mention of his name. (OP, Ch. 5) When Ron makes a mildly funny remark about Goyle, Luna Lovegood reacts with prolonged laughter, as if the comment was *hysterical*. (OP, Ch. 10)

Prominent - Noticeable or sticking out. Umbridge has prominent eyes. (OP, Ch. 11) Prof. Grubbly-Plank has a prominent chin. (GF, Ch. 24)

Prone - Have a tendency. As the date that Harry would return to Hogwarts approached, Sirius became prone to being *taciturn* and sad. (OP, Ch. 24)

Pronounced - Well-defined, prominent. As Voldemort and Wormtail discuss Bertha Jorkins, the cruelness in Voldemort's voice become more pronounced. (GF, Ch. 1)

Pronouncements - Statements of authority. Voldemort says he has seen no evidence to support Dumbledore's pronouncements that love is more powerful than dark magic. (HBP, Ch. 20)

Proportions - Size, dimensions. While Harry is quite impressed at how much space their is inside the Weasleys' enchanted tent at the Quidditch World Cup, Ron does not seem to find the tent's inner proportions at all remarkable. (GF, Ch. 7)

Proprietor - Shop owner. Harry hears the proprietor of Quality Quidditch Supplies brag that the Irish team had ordered Firebolts. (PA, Ch. 4)

Proscribed - Banned. The reason that one cannot buy a flying carpet in England is they are on the Ministry of Magic's Registry of Proscribed Charmable Objects. (GF, Ch. 7)

Prospect - Future opportunity. The prospect of speaking face-to-face with Sirius is all that sustained Harry before the first task in the Triwizard Tournament. (GF, Ch. 19)

Prostrating - Lying down in a desperate appeal. Winky responds to Barty Crouch's threat of giving her clothes by prostrating herself at his feet. (GF, Ch. 9) One of the Death Eaters tells the restored Voldemort that he prostrates himself before the Dark Lord, and Voldemort says, "That will do." (GF, Ch. 33)

Prototype - The first of a new product. Harry sees a prototype of the Firebolt at Quality Quidditch Supplies. (PA, Ch. 4)

Protracted - Long. After Wormtail suggests Lord Voldemort could accomplish his goal without attacking Harry Potter, there is a protracted silence. (GF, Ch. 1) After George demonstrates use of a Skiving Snackbox, vomiting and then recovering, there is protracted applause. (OP, Ch. 17)

Protruding - Sticking out. Stan Shunpike has protruding ears. (PA, Ch. 2) In the Dark Mark, a serpent is seen protruding from the mouth of a skull. (GF, Ch. 9)

Protuberance - A nose or something else that sticks out. Tonks demonstrates her ability to change her appearance by changing her nose into a beaklike protuberance. (OP, Ch. 5)

Protuberant - Prominent, sticking out. Luna has protuberant eyes. (HBP, Ch. 15)

Provocation - Something that prompts one to speak or act. Harry avoids Seamus Finnigan one evening because he feels could not deal with any more provocation. (OP, Ch. 13)

Provoking - Prompting. Harry tries to anger Ron as a way of provoking him to adopt a *defiant*, goal-saving attitude, but this *strategy* doesn't work. (HBP, Ch. 14)

Prowess - Skill. The Triwizard Tournament is a test of wizardly prowess. (GF, Ch. 16)

Prudent - Cautious. Slughorn says that since Voldemort has resurfaced, he thinks it is prudent to keep a low profile. (HBP, Ch. 4)

Publicity - Coverage in newspapers and other media. The Prime Minister tells Fudge that the murder of Amelia Bones was *baffling* to Muggle police and had been getting a lot of publicity. (HBP, Ch. 1)

Puce - A dark red color. Uncle Vernon's face sometimes turns puce when he's angry (PA, Ch. 2).

Pulsating - Throbbing. Hermione drops a pulsating pod in Herbology, but Prof. Sprout urges her to squeeze it while it is fresh. (HBP, Ch. 14)

Pummeling - Punching. Harry is pummeling his pillow in anger and frustration after people assume that he told a snake to attack another student in the dueling club. (CS, Ch. 11)

Punch-drunk - Woozy; behaving as if one had been hit on the head. Ron has so much trouble waking up one morning at The Burrow that he looks slightly punch-drunk. (HBP, Ch. 5)

Punctuated - Interrupted. Harry chooses not to tell Mr. Weasley about his scar hurting because he doesn't want his visit to the Quidditch World Cup punctuated with questions about how his forehead felt. (GF, Ch. 2)

Punctured - With a hole. Harry sees a punctured football that had been used as a Portkey. (GF, Ch. 7)

Pungent - Strong-smelling. As Harry flies down to 12 Grimmauld Place, he sees garbage bags and smells their pungent odor. (OP, Ch. 3)

Pursuits - Activities. The night before a Quidditch match between Slytherin and Gryffindor, all typical pursuits stopped in the Gryffindor common room; even Hermione put down her books. (PA, Ch. 15)

Putrid - Stinking. Harry smells a dementor's putrid, death-cold breath. (OP, Ch. 1)

Quailing - Cowering, losing one's courage. Hermione says she really prefers Prof. Grubbly-Plank as a teacher but, quailing under Harry's furious stare, she quickly adds that she does want Hagrid back. (GF, Ch. 24)

Quaking - Shaking. In Tom Riddle's closet in the orphanage, there is a quaking box containing stolen items. (HBP, Ch. 13)

Quash - Suppress, hold down. After Ron contacts Percy regarding their suspicions about Mr. Crouch, Percy writes that he is too busy to quash ridiculous rumors. (GF, Ch. 28)

Quavering - Trembling sound. Fawkes emits a quavering note that strengthens Harry. (GF, Ch. 36)

Queasy - Slightly sick to one's stomach. Mad-Eye Moody's magical eye can swivel around so fast it makes Harry queasy to watch it. (GF, Ch. 20)

Quelled - Quieted. Laughter in Snape's class was quelled by a look the professor gave. (HBP, Ch. 21)

Query - Question. Ron's query about where the Durmstrang students would sleep was answered when Karkaroff ordered everyone back to their ship. (GF, Ch. 16)

Queue (pronounced "kyu") - Line of people waiting. At the Quidditch World Cup, Harry sees a queue of people lined up at a *tap*. (GF, Ch. 7)

Queuing (pronounced "kyu-ing") - Lining up. The entrance hall is packed with people queuing for dinner when Malfoy tells Ron in a loud voice that he ought to read what *The Daily Prophet* says about his father. (GF, Ch. 13)

Quibbling - Arguing over a very insignificant point. Percy is offended by Rita Skeeter's contention that the Ministry is wasting its time by quibbling over cauldron thickness. (GF, Ch. 10)

Quivering - Shaking. When Dobby secretly visits Harry at Hogwarts, his ears are quivering when he hears footsteps. (CS, Ch. 10) Dumbledore's mustache is quivering when he observes that Gilderoy Lockhart's memory-erasing charm backfired. (CS, Ch. 18)

Quizzical - Questioning, puzzled. Cedric gives Harry a quizzical look before they are attacked by Death Eaters. (GF, Ch. 32)

Radiant - Glowing. Hermione is radiant after she hears Slughorn repeat Harry's comment that she is the best in their Hogwarts' class. (HBP, Ch. 9)

Rampaging - Running wild. After Hermione notices that Ron wrote in his Divination homework that he would drown twice, he yawns and decides to change one of the drownings to being trampled by a rampaging hippogriff. (GF, Ch. 14)

Rancid - Stinking. When Neville pokes a Mimbulus mimbletonia plant, it emits green jets of slime that smell like rancid manure. (OP, Ch. 10)

Rangy - Long-limbed. The Prime Minister sees that Rufus Scrimgeour has a rangy, *loping* grace. (HBP, Ch. 1)

Ransacked - Rummaged through and stolen from. Harry felt as if his brain had been ransacked after he was named a Triwizard champion. (GF, Ch. 17)

Rant - A longwinded complaint. Harry ignores Uncle Vernon's rant about how awful owls are. (OP, Ch. 2)

Ranting - Complaining, criticizing or protesting in a longwinded way. Hagrid is ranting about how Harry is innocent of attacks on Hogwarts students until Dumbledore says he does not suspect Harry. (CS, Ch. 12) The Prime Minister is disturbed when Cornelius Fudge bursts into his office from the fireplace, ranting about "Serious" Black and a boy named Harry Potter. (HBP, Ch. 1)

Rapt - Completely absorbed. Hagrid talks to Madame Maxime with a rapt expression. (GF, Ch. 16) Voldemort looks rapt and *exultant* when his body is restored. (GF, Ch. 33)

Rasp - A rough, unpleasant sound. After he drinks Polyjuice Potion, Harry finds his voice is a low rasp, just like Goyle's. (CS, Ch. 12)

Raucous - Noisy and disorderly. The mandrakes hold a loud and raucous party in greenhouse three, which makes Prof. Sprout think they soon will be mature. (CS, Ch. 15) Harry sees raucous dwarfs in the Leaky Cauldron. (PA, Ch. 4) The Slytherins are full of raucous laughter when Draco mimes the breaking of Harry's nose. (HBP, Ch. 8) Harry and Dumbledore hear raucous shouting outside the Three Broomsticks as they see Madame Rosmerta *ejecting* a wizard. (HBP, Ch. 25)

Ravine - A v-shaped slope worn down by running water. In Gringotts Bank, the car that Harry and Hagrid ride with Griphook crosses a ravine. (SS, Ch. 6)

Raving - Talking irrationally, in a frenzy. After Umbridge accuses Prof. McGonagall of wanting to become headmistress of Hogwarts and Dumbledore to become Minister of Magic, McGonagall tells Umbridge, "You are raving." (OP, Ch. 29)

Realization - Moment of understanding. When Harry reached the realization that Hagrid had forced a giant to leave his home to come to the Forbidden Forest, he uttered a small gasp of horror. (OP, Ch. 30)

Reanimated - Brought back to life. Snape tells his class that an Inferious is a corpse that a dark wizard has reanimated. (HBP, Ch. 21)

Reassurance - Soothing information. Rita Skeeter writes that wizard who needed reassurance after the appearance of the Dark Mark didn't get it from the Ministry of Magic. (GF, Ch. 10) In their first meeting, Cornelius Fudge gave the Prime Minister reassurances that he need not know about the affairs of the wizarding community, because the Ministry of Magic takes full responsibility for it. (HBP, Ch. 1)

Rebellious - Opposing authority. Hermione suggests taking the night off, explaining she feels a bit rebellious. (OP, Ch. 28)

Rebound - Bounce off. Voldemort's curse rebounds off Harry and injures Voldemort. (PA, Ch. 1)

Rebuffed - Rejected. Sir Cadogan attempts to move into another portrait but is rebuffed by a dog. (OP, Ch. 12)

Recede - Move or fade away. Harry's problems seem to recede as he realizes he is about to return to the wizarding world. (OP, Ch. 3)

Receptivity - Ability to sense; also, an attitude of welcoming. Prof. Trelawney tells Hermione that she has "very little receptivity to the *resonances* of the future." (PA, Ch. 6)

Rechristened - Renamed. Buckbeak is rechristened as "Witherwings." (HBP, Ch. 3)

Reckon - Assume or guess. When Snape seems to avoid Mad-Eye Moody, Harry says, "I reckon Snape's a bit scared of him." (GF, Ch. 14) Ron asks Hermione, "You reckon Ludo Bagman *conjured* the Dark Mark?" (GF, Ch. 27)

Recounting - Telling others about a series of events. Harry imagines he hears Slytherins laughing and that Malfoy is recounting how he discovered and attacked Harry in their carriage on the Hogwarts Express. (HBP, Ch. 8)

Recruiting - Seeking someone for a role or job. Slughorn gives Dumbledore a dirty look when the headmaster suggests Death Eaters would be interested in recruiting him. (HBP, Ch. 4)

Recurrence - Happening again. While taking for an OWL in History of Magic, Harry puzzles over a question about a how a secrecy law was broken and what was done to prevent a recurrence. (OP, Ch. 31)

Redolent - Full of an odor or atmosphere. Kreacher gave Sirius a look that was redolent of the deepest *loathing*. (OP, Ch. 6)

Redoubled - Increased one's effort. Harry redoubled his grip while appa-rating with Dumbledore. (HBP, Ch. 4)

Reformed - Gave up a bad way of life. Sirius tells Snape that while Dumbledore might believe that Snape has reformed after being a death eater, he doesn't. (OP, Ch. 24)

Refuge - A safe place. When it becomes obvious that Harry is about to talk about magic, Uncle Vernon interrupts him and takes refuge in read-ing a letter. (GF, Ch. 3)

Regally - Like royalty. When Harry and his friends encounter Neville's grandmother at St. Mungo's, they notice that she *proffered* her hand regally. (OP, Ch. 23)

Registry - Official list. One cannot buy a flying carpet in England because they are on the Ministry of Magic's Registry of Proscribed Charmable Objects. (GF, Ch. 7)

Regurgitate - Vomit or spit out. Mr. Weasley says that a wizard has been making Muggle toilets regurgitate when flushed, and that Muggle plumbers are *flummoxed* about the cause. (OP, Ch. 7) The Goblet of Fire regurgitated Harry's name. (GF, Ch. 21)

Reimburse - Repay. Ron promised to reimburse Harry for an elixir to improve his ability to think during exams, but Hermione *confiscated* it. (OP, Ch. 31)

Reinforce - Support. To reinforce her insistence that Harry stop claim-ing that Voldemort had returned, Umbridge forces Harry to write lines with a magic pen that cuts his hand. (OP, Ch. 13)

Reinstate - Restart after an absence. Dumbledore says there have been many attempts to reinstate the TriWizard Tournament. (GF, Ch. 12) Dumbledore is reinstated as head of the Wizengamot. (HBP, Ch. 3)

Rekindled - Relit, or brought back into existence. The lights go out when the boggart turns into a dementor, but are rekindled after it disappears. (PA, Ch. 11)

Relapse - To fall back to an old pattern of behavior. Snape says Dumbledore refused to give him the Defense Against the Dark Arts job because he was afraid it might cause him to relapse "into my old ways." (HBP, Ch. 2)

Relevant - Relates to what you're talking about. When researching the defense of Buckbeak, Harry, Ron and Hermione look for anything relevant in books about cases of *marauding* beasts. (PA, Ch. 11)

Relish - Delight. Rita Skeeter sucks on her Quick-Quotes Quill with apparent relish. (GF, Ch. 18)

Reluctant - Resisting the idea of doing a certain task. After Snape asks Filch to help him search for an *intruder* who broke into his office, Filch appears reluctant to *forgo* the chance to catch Peeves instead. (GF, Ch. 25) Dumbledore says that Kreacher has shown a reluctance to have Harry become his new owner. (HBP, Ch. 3)

Rematerialize - Reappear. Harry is able to disappear and rematerialize after learning to apparate, but he prefers flying. (HBP, Ch. 21)

Reminisce (verb) - Recall. Dumbledore says that it has been almost impossible to find anyone who can reminisce about Voldemort. (HBP, Ch. 20) Mrs. Weasley reminisces about Ogg, the gamekeeper before Hagrid. (GF, Ch. 31)

Reminiscences - Memories. Snape says he served the Dark Lord by spying on Dumbledore while all Bellatrix LeStrange could offer were endless reminiscences of life in Azkaban. (HBP, Ch. 2)

Reminiscent - Reminding of. Hermione gave Ron a look that was reminiscent of Prof. McGonagall. (GF, Ch. 12)

Remonstration - Protest by argument. After Ron confiscates Fanged Frisbee and happily says that he always wanted one, Hermione's remonstration is drowned out by Lavender Brown's laughter. (HBP, Ch. 9)

Remorse - Regret. Snape says that after the Dark Lord disappeared, he told Dumbledore a tale of having deep remorse for having supported Voldemort. (HBP, Ch. 2)

Remotely - Faintly. After Dumbledore reminds Rita Skeeter that she has called him an "obsolete dingbat" in print, she doesn't look even remotely *abashed*. (GF, Ch. 18) The Prime Minister was not remotely pleased to see Cornelius Fudge. (HBP, Ch. 1) After Dumbledore tells a young Tom Riddle that he knows he is a thief, Riddle does not seem even remotely *abashed*. (HBP, Ch. 13)

Rendered - Gave. Firenze says Hagrid has rendered him a great service. (OP, Ch. 27)

Renown - High reputation. The Sorting Hat sings in Book 4 that Hogwarts was founded by four wizards of renown. (GF, Ch. 12)

Repel - Push away. Beaters use bats to repel bludgers. (PA, Ch. 8)

Replenish - Resupply. Harry replenishes his potions ingredients by visiting an *apothecary* on Diagon Alley. (PA, Ch. 4)

Replicas - Close copies or reproductions. Harry recalls using Polyjuice Potion, which turned him and Ron into replicas of Crabbe and Goyle. (GF, Ch. 25) Voldemort rewards Wormtail by giving him a replica of the hand he cut off. (GF, Ch. 33)

Repose - Place. *The Daily Prophet* quotes an anonymous Ministry of Magic official as saying that Dolores Umbridge's appointment as High Inquisitor is a step toward ensuring that Hogwarts has a headmaster "in whom we can all repose confidence." (OP, Ch. 15)

Repossessed - Regained. Oliver Wood becomes repossessed of his enthusiasm for Quidditch in December after losing to Hufflepuff earlier in the year. (PA, Ch. 10)

Repressively - In a manner to silence, hold down or hold back. When students ask about Hagrid, Prof. Grubbly-Plank says, repressively, "Never you mind." (OP, Ch. 13)

Reprimand - A punishment in the form of words. Harry wonders if he will receive a reprimand from Dumbledore when he tells him that he fell asleep in Divination class. (GF, Ch. 30)

Reprimanded - Scolded. Harry is unsure whether he is being reprimanded when Dumbledore says Harry should have questioned him to make sure that he was not an *imposter*. (HBP, Ch. 4)

Reproachfully - With an air of criticism. Hedwig gazes at Harry reproachfully when Harry demands the owl abandon a meal to deliver a message. (OP, Ch. 3)

Reprovingly - In a manner to express disapproval. After Fred calls Snape a "git," Hermione stares at him reprovingly and reminds him that Snape is a member of the Order of the Phoenix. (OP, Ch. 4)

Repugnant - Unlikable and *contrary* to one's values. Harry finds it repugnant to think about Kreacher possibly falling into the possession Bellatrix LeStrange, who murdered Sirius. (HBP, Ch. 3)

Repulsive - So disgusting that it drives one away. Blast-ended skrewts have suckers, stingers and fire-blasting ends, making them the most repulsive things Harry ever saw. (GF, Ch. 21)

Resemblance - Similarity. Snape says the resemblance between Harry and his father is *uncanny*, because they are both *arrogant*. (PA, Ch. 14)

Resentful - Upset about an event viewed as unjust. Draco Malfoy is resentful after his father is removed from the Board of Governors of Hogwarts. (CS, Ch. 18).

Residue - Remainder. Harry's trunk is empty except for a residue of miscellaneous items. (HBP, Ch. 3)

Resolutely - In a determined way. After Hermione calls the Quibbler "rubbish," Luna informs her that Luna's father is the editor and resolutely returns to reading it. (OP, Ch. 10) Horace Slughorn turns away from Harry resolutely, as if to say he won't be tempted by Dumbledore's offer to teach at Hogwarts. (HBP, Ch. 4) When Dumbledore brings up the subject of Sirius Black, Harry stares resolutely at a spider climbing up Dumbledore's hat. (HBP, Ch. 4) Hermione resolutely refuses to help Harry with work, knowing he would just share it with Ron. (HBP, Ch. 20)

Resonances - Vibrations or other sensations that, like an echo, relate to a past or future event. Prof. Trelawney tells Hermonie that she has "very little *receptivity* to the resonances of the future." (PA, Ch. 6)

Resorting - Using something as a backup. In a Quidditch match, Slytherin players resort to dirty play such as hitting opposing players. (PA, Ch. 15)

Respite - Rest. On a rainy day, the changing rooms at the Quidditch pitch are a respite from the bad weather. (OP, Ch. 18)

Resplendent - Shining splendidly. Gilderoy Lockhart looks resplendent in his plum-colored robes. (CS, Ch. 11)

Resounding - Loud, strong. Applause for Viktor Krum after the Quidditch World Cup is resounding. (GF, Ch. 8)

Restive - Fidgety, difficult to deal with. Hagrid says Aragog has been restive. (HBP, Ch. 11)

Resultant - Resulting. After a loud crack indicates that someone has disapparated on Privet Drive, Harry bangs his head on a windowsill; the resultant crash makes Aunt Petunia shriek all the louder. (OP, Ch. 1)

Resurgence - Coming again. When Hermione tells Umbridge she has a message for Dumbledore, Harry sees a resurgence of Umbridge's interest. (OP, Ch. 32)

Retaliation - Getting someone back. After a Slytherin Quidditch beater hits Alicia Spinnet of Gryffindor with his club, George Weasley elbows the other player in the face in retaliation. (PA, Ch. 15)

Retort (verb) - Argue in reply. When Riddle claims the mere memory of him had driven Dumbledore away, Harry retorts that Dumbledore is not as gone as Riddle thinks. (CS, Ch. 17)

Retorts (noun, plural) - Challenging replies. Harry imagines that Vernon Dursley can think of many retorts to Albus Dumbledore, but the wizard's wand intimidates him. (HBP, Ch. 3)

Retreated - Backed away. Before paying for a campground at the Quidditch World Cup, Mr. Weasley retreated to ask Harry about Muggle money. (GF, Ch. 7)

Retribution - Punishment. Draco threatens Mr. Borgin with retribution if he tells anyone about what Draco is interested in. (HBP, Ch. 6)

Retrieve - Get something back. Harry didn't dare retrieve his invisibility cloak from below the statue of the one-eyed witch. (PA, Ch. 16)

Reverberate - Vibrate or echo. When Harry falls into the pensieve and finds himself in a courtroom, he lets out a cry that reverberates in the silent room. (GF, Ch. 30) When Fred and George arrange a diversion, screams reverberate in the halls. (OP, Ch. 29) After Dumbledore dies, Fawkes's sorrowful song reverberates over the Hogwarts grounds. (HBP, Ch. 27)

Revere - Honor, hold in high regard. Slughorn tells Hagrid that not only is he interested in creatures like Aragog, but that he reveres them. (HBP, Ch. 22)

Reverence - Deep respect and adoration. Hagrid looks upon the Hungarian Horntail with something close to reverence. (GF, Ch. 19) Dumbledore says that had Lucius Malfoy known that Tom Riddle's diary actually contained a piece of his master's soul, he would have treated it with more reverence. (HBP, Ch. 23)

Reverie - State of deep thought. Barty Crouch comes out of a reverie to give the four Triwizard champions their instructions. (GF, Ch. 17) Harry notices that Hermione goes into a reverie after Ron suggests that Order of the Phoenix Member Sturgis Podmore might have been set up before his arrest for allegedly breaking into the Ministry of Magic. (OP, Ch. 14) A crash brings Harry out of his reverie as he stares at the Marauder's Map. (HBP, Ch. 24)

Reverted - Returned to a former state or condition. Slughorn treated Harry coldly after Harry asked about him about Horcruxes, but reverted to his usual friendly manner after a while. (HBP, Ch. 18)

Reverting - Going back. After Harry stopped taking Occlumency lessons, Hermione refused to drop the subject and kept reverting to it. (OP, Ch. 30)

Revolt - Disgust. Lord Voldemort tells Wormtail, "I revolt you." (GF, Ch. 1)

Rhapsodizing - Speaking in a highly emotional way, like a musical rhapsody. Ron rhapsodizes to anyone who will listen about his new broomstick. (OP, Ch. 9)

Rickety - Unstable. In Prof. Trelawney's classroom, Harry, Ron and Hermione all sit at the same rickety table. (PA, Ch. 15)

Rife - Widespread. *The Daily Prophet* reports that "*speculation* is rife" that a disturbance at the Hall of Prophecy involved a prophecy about Harry Potter. (HBP, Ch. 3)

Rift - Split. *The Daily Prophet* reports rumors of a rift between Albus Dumbledore and Rufus Scrimgeour, the new Minister of Magic. (HBP, Ch. 3)

Robustly - With great fullness. Ron robustly dismisses Harry's concern that it might be wrong for him to want to *retrieve* the Half Blood Prince's book from where he stashed in the Room of Requirement. (HBP, Ch. 25)

Rogue - A lone, unpredictable *marauder,* or a dishonest person who's up to no good, or a mischief-maker. In a Quidditch match against Slytherin, Harry is attacked by a wild bludger that is described as a rogue. (CS, Ch. 10) Sir Cadogan calls Harry a rogue until he understands that Harry is not making fun of him and is lost (PA, Ch. 6).

Roguish - Playful and a bit naughty. After Gilderoy Lockhart hints that he would like a large bottle of Ogden's Old Firewhisky as a birthday gift, he gives the class a roguish wink. (CS, Ch. 6)

Rotund - Round, chubby. Harry sees in the pensieve that Slughorn was rotund even when he was young. (HBP, Ch. 17)

Roused - Awakened. Ron mutters some words *indistinctly* when roused by his mother. (GF, Ch. 6) Dumbledore's warm greeting of Harry appears to rouse Uncle Vernon, who had been silent. (HBP, Ch. 3)

Roving - Moving around. Harry sees Prof. Trelawney's enormous eyes roving around the table, counting the number of people gathered, until she realizes that she would make 13. (PA, Ch. 11)

Row - In England, an argument. Harry worries that a row between Mrs. Weasley and the twins over their joke shop could lead to a Percy-like *estrangement.* (OP, Ch. 9)

Ruddy - In England, something that is intensely disliked; also used to describe a face with a healthy, reddish glow. Uncle Vernon tells Harry, "I'll sign your ruddy form." (PA, Ch. 2) On the day of Buckbeak's scheduled execution, Hagrid's face lost its ruddy glow. (PA, Ch. 16) Uncle Vernon is so annoyed by wine glasses that Dumbledore has conjured that he yells, "Would you get these ruddy things off us?" (HBP, Ch. 3)

Rudimentary - Basic. Voldemort says he gave instructions to Wormtail on how to restore him to a rudimentary, weak body until he could be fully restored. (GF, Ch. 33)

Ruefully - In a way that inspires pity. Cho Chang says ruefully that she was casting a defensive charm well until Harry showed up and made her nervous. (OP, Ch. 18) Hermione ruefully informs Fred Weasley that his punching telescope gave her a black eye. (HBP, Ch. 6)

Rummaging - Searching through. The Prime Minister notices Rufus Scrimgeour rummaging through his pockets for floo powder. (HBP, Ch. 1)

Ruse - Trick accomplished by misdirecting someone's attention. When announcing a Quidditch match, Luna Lovegood says the fact that that Harry is arguing with his goalkeeper could be a clever ruse. (HBP, Ch. 19)

Ruthlessly - Without mercy, with single-minded determination. Ruthlessly, Bellatrix LeStrange tells her sister, Narcissa, that she ought to be proud to have Draco serve the Dark Lord, even if it costs him his life. (HBP, Ch. 2)

Sacked - In England, fired from a job. Lucius Malfoy tried to get Hagrid sacked. (GF, Ch. 15) Cornelius Fudge informs the Prime Minister that Fudge has been sacked and replaced by Rufus Scrimgeour. (HBP, Ch. 1) Hermione says that if Barty Crouch looks ill, it's just his *comeuppance* for sacking Winky. (GF, Ch. 27)

Sallow - A grayish, unhealthy yellow. Snape is described as having sallow skin, (PA, Ch. 14)

Sanctimoniously - In a way that conveys that one is superior, although others do not perceive this to be true. Percy Weasley sanctimoniously states he hopes the World Cup does not last five days because his important duties at the Ministry of Magic would pile up. (GF, Ch. 5)

Sarcastically - In a way that suggests a person is not sincere in expressing a feeling or idea, and often means the opposite. About blast-ended screwts, Malfoy says, sarcastically, "Who wouldn't want pets that can burn, sting and bite all at once?" (GF, Ch. 13)

Sardonically - In a sarcastic and mocking way. Snape repeats what Bellatrix says sardonically. (HBP, Ch. 2)

Saturated - Soaked. A month before exams, Harry's brain felt saturated with information. (OP, Ch. 30)

Savagely - Fiercely and cruelly. After Harry's secret trip to Hogsmeade ends in disaster, Ron says savagely to Hermione, "Come to have a good gloat?" (PA, Ch. 14) When Rita Skeeter asks for a word with Harry after the first task of the Triwizard competition, he says savagely, "Yeah, you can have a word. Goodbye." (GF, Ch. 20)

Savoring - Enjoying greatly a taste or experience. The Prime Minister is standing in his office, savoring his victory in winning his post, when he hears a portrait cough for the first time. (HBP, Ch. 1)

Scabbard - Holder for a sword, usually worn on a belt. After Sir Cadogan pulls his heavy sword out of its scabbard, he has trouble maintaining his balance. (PA, Ch. 6)

Scalawag - An affectionate term for a wrong-doer. When Harry spends a detention helping Gilderoy Lockhart answer his fan mail, Lockhart greets by saying, "Ah, here's the scalawag. (CS, Ch. 7)

Scalding - Hot enough to burn, or close to it. Harry and Ron drink scalding tea in Divination. (PA, Ch. 6)

Scampering - Running fast and playfully. Fang scampers in the Forbidden Forest with Harry and Ron. (CS, Ch. 15)

Scandalized - Shocked and offended. Hermione looks scandalized when Ron suggests she drop a couple of subjects. (PA, Ch. 12) Parvati and Lavender look scandalized when Ron cracks jokes at Prof. Trelawney's expense. (PA, Ch. 15) Hermione looks scandalized when she sees Ron drinking what she thought was Felix Felicis. (HBP, Ch. 14)

Scarlet woman - A woman considered morally bad because she is intimate with many men. Hermione responds to lies about her relationship with Harry by laughing, but Ron is concerned that she has been portrayed as a scarlet woman. (GF, Ch. 27)

Scathingly - In a severe way. Uncle Vernon doesn't believe that Harry is interested in the Muggle news, and scathingly asks Aunt Petunia what he is up to. (OP, Ch. 1)

Scoffed - Spoke in a disrespectful, sneering way. Hermione scoffed when Ron claimed to be concerned about Winky, the house elf. (GF, Ch. 28)

Scorn - View something as ridiculous or unworthy. Sir Cadogan wonders if Harry, Ron and Hermione are staring at his painting because he has fallen off his horse: "Come to scorn at my fall, perchance?" (PA, Ch. 5)

Scrounger - A person who asks others for money or goods. Aunt Marge describes James Potter as a "no-account, good-for-nothing, lazy scrounger." (PA, Ch. 2).

Scrum - A group of people all trying to get at something, like rugby players going for the ball. When Dobby tipped the D.A. off that Umbridge was coming, everyone ran for the door, forming a scrum. (OP, Ch. 27)

Scrutinizing - Examining closely. At the site of the Quidditch World Cup, a Muggle named Mr. Roberts appears to be scrutinizing Mr. Weasley, who seems confused about how to pay a bill in Muggle money. (GF, Ch. 7)

Scumbag - An offensive term for a person viewed as dishonest or immoral. After Karkaroff judges Harry as earning only four of 10 possible points for getting an egg protected by a Hungarian Horntail, Ron shouts out this insult, which is probably the most offensive term in the Harry Potter series. (GF, Ch. 20)

Scurvy - Lousy, despicable. Sir Cadogan calls Harry a "scurvy braggart" until he understands that Harry and his friends are lost and needs help. (PA, Ch. 6) When Sir Cadogan is on duty in the portrait hole, the password at one point is "scurvy *cur*." (PA, Ch. 11)

Scuttled - Moved quickly. Spiders scuttle together to a meeting place on the Hogwart's grounds, then head for the Forbidden Forest. (CS, Ch. 15) The Monster Book of Monsters scuttles sideways, "like some weird crab." (PA, Ch. 1)

Secateurs - In England, pruning shears. Ron beats back a Snargaluff plant in Herbology with a pair of secateurs. (HBP, Ch. 14)

Secluded - Out of the way. Harry, Ron and Hermione choose a secluded spot to talk about what Snape might teach in the first potions lesson of year five. (OP, Ch. 12)

Sedately - Calmly, quietly. Harry and Hermione slow down to walk sedately past their examiners in the fifth year. (OP, Ch. 31)

Segregation - Keeping separate. Hermione thinks werewolf segregation is a dumb idea. (OP, Ch. 9)

Seizure - An attack that makes one temporarily lose control of one's body. Just before Prof. Trelawney issues a prophecy that a servant will join the Dark Lord, making him more powerful, she appears to have a seizure. (PA, Ch. 16)

Selfsame - Identical. The Sorting Hat sings in year five that the founders of Hogwarts all had the "selfsame yearning" — to create the best school of magic. (OP, Ch. 11)

Senile - Losing one's ability to reason due to old age. *The Daily Prophet* promotes the view that Harry is a liar and Dumbledore is going senile. (OP, Ch. 13)

Sensational - Exciting great interest. Prof. Binns says the legend of the Chamber of Secrets is a "sensational, even *ludicrous* tale." (CS, Ch. 9) Slughorn calls the story of the prophecy about Harry sensational and asks about it. (HBP, Ch. 7)

Sensitivity - Anticipation of and compassion for other's feelings. After Ron makes a joke at the expense of Nearly Headless Nick, the ghost says, "Once again, you show all the sensitivity of a blunt axe." (HBP, Ch. 8)

Sentiments - Feelings. After Dumbledore says his removal from Hogwarts will not stop people from being loyal to him, Lucius Malfoy says, "Admirable sentiments," in a falsely gracious way. (CS, Ch. 15)

Sepulchral - Like a funeral. A wizard named Bode greets Mr. Weasley in a sepulchral voice. (OP, Ch. 7)

Sequined - Decorated with small, shiny circles. Prof. Trelawney wore a green, sequined dress to a Christmas meal, "making her look more than ever like a glittering, oversized dragonfly." (PA, Ch. 11)

Serenely - Calmly, peacefully. Dumbledore smiles serenely when explaining to Lucius Malfoy why he is back at Hogwarts even though the Board of Governors had voted to suspend him. (CS, Ch. 18) Luna speaks serenely when fondly remembering the D.A. (HBP, Ch. 7)

Serpentine - Snake-like. Inside the Chamber of Secrets, Harry moves among serpentine columns. (CS, Ch. 17)

Servility - State of being a slave or available to serve others. Seeing a statue of a house elf, Harry thinks it captures the attitude of servility that he has seen in house elves. (OP, Ch. 9)

Servitude - State of working for others as a servant. Bane says Firenze has disgraced himself by entering into "servitude to humans" by working at Hogwarts. (OP, Ch. 30)

Sever - Cut. Percy urges Ron to sever ties with Harry because there is a *stigma* that comes with associating with allies of Dumbledore (OP, Ch. 14)

Sheepish - Embarrassed. Ron looks sheepish when Harry asks him to please stop pretending to be asleep when Lavender visits him in the hospital wing. (HBP, Ch. 19)

Shortlisted - Made a finalist for a desirable position. Dumbledore said the heads of Beaubatons and Durmstrang will be arriving with shortlisted students, one of whom will be selected to represent each of their schools in the Triwizard Tournament. (OP, Ch. 12)

Shrewdly - With a keen understanding of the situation. Fred shrewdly picks apart what Dumbledore said about how the Triwizard champions will be selected, looking for a way to enter his name into the competition even though he is too young. (GF, Ch. 12) Dumbledore shrewdly guesses that Harry did not pack his trunk because he was doubtful that Dumbledore would turn up at Privet Drive. (HBP, Ch. 3)

Shrewdness - Ability to size up a situation well. Rufus Scrimgeour impresses the Prime Minister as having the quality of shrewdness. (HBP, Ch. 1)

Shrilly - In a high voice. Mrs. Weasley speaks shrilly when arguing with her husband about how much Harry needs to know about Sirius Black. (PA, Ch. 4) Dobby shrilly declares that he is free. (CS, Ch. 18) Moaning Myrtle protests shrilly when Harry talks about breathing in front of her, saying this is *tactless*. (GF, Ch. 25)

Shufti - A quick look around. Ron says that if one encounters what may be an Inferius, a shufti would be in order to see if it's transparent — and therefore a ghost — rather than engage it in conversation. (HBP, Ch. 21)

Shunted - Moved to one side. Harry avoids conversing with Colin Creevy because they are shunted in opposite directions by the *throng* of students in the corridor. (CS, Ch. 9)

Skeptical - Doubting. Ron looks skeptical when Hermione says that his brothers Fred and George would never break the law in order to acquire gold. (GF, Ch. 29)

Skulking - Moving as if not to be noticed, as if a coward. Harry notices Dudley skulking behind his parents during Dumbledore's visit to Privet Drive. (HBP, Ch. 3)

Sidle - Move or turn sideways. Hagrid is so big he must sidle through doorways. (SS, Ch. 17)

Silhouette - Outline. Harry sees the silhouette of an enormous, shaggy dog in the sky while playing Quidditch. (PA, Ch. 9)

Simper - A smirk or silly smile. When Umbridge speaks, it's often with a simper. (OP, Ch. 8)

Simpering - Smirking. Umbridge has a fussy, simpering *demeanor*. (OP, Ch. 29)

Single-handedly - Describes something done without help. Hagrid single-handedly delivers 12 Christmas trees to the Great Hall. (HBP, Ch. 15)

Sinister - Evil. Thestrals look sinister. (OP, Ch. 10)

Skein - A coil of thread or yarn. Slughorn is attracted by a skein of hair that he sees in Hagrid's hut and recognizes as unicorn hair. (HBP, Ch. 22)

Skeptical - Doubting, disbelieving. Ron is skeptical of Harry's claim that he did not place his name in the Goblet of Fire. (GF, Ch. 17)

Skirting - Avoiding, moving on the edge. Harry notices people skirting around him in the hallways amid rumors that he is the heir of Slytherin. (CS, Ch. 12)

Skive - Shave. Fred teases Ron, "Hogwarts prefects surely don't wish to skive off lessons." (OP, Ch. 12)

Skulking - Moving in a quiet, secretive way. Mrs. Norris is seen skulking near the forbidden third floor. (SS, Ch. 13)

Slander - False statements about a person that injure his or her reputation. After Cornelius Fudge reports that Voldemort has returned, *The Daily Prophet* reports that Harry Potter stuck to his story and endured slander. (OP, Ch. 37)

Sleek - Smooth and attractive. Harry observes that Lucius Malfoy's usually sleek hair was *disheveled*. (CS, Ch. 18)

Sluggishly - Slowly. The Polyjuice Potion bubbles sluggishly. (CS, Ch. 12)

Smarmiest - Gushing with self-admiration more than anyone else. Ron asks, "Is Lockhart the smarmiest *bloke* you've ever met, or what?" (CS, Ch. 13)

Smitten - Taken over by feelings of affection and longing. Rita Skeeter writes that Viktor Krum is smitten with the "*devious*" Hermione Granger. (GF, Ch. 27)

Smoldering - Burning slowly and emitting smoke, like a heap of ashes. After Fawkes bursts into flames, all that's left is a smoldering pile of ashes. (CS, Ch. 12)

Smugness - Feeling of self-satisfaction and superiority. Uncle Vernon's face is full of smugness when he tells Harry that he, Aunt Petunia and Dudley will be going out; he doesn't realize that the notice he received about winning a lawn maintenance award was a fake *concocted* by members of the Order of the Phoenix (OP, Ch. 3)

Snide - Mean-spirited. *The Daily Prophet* prints snide *allusions* to Harry. (OP, Ch. 14)

Sniggering - Laughing cruelly and secretively, sometimes behind one's hand. Percy wonders what everyone is sniggering about after Fred and George bewitch his prefect badge so that it reads, "Pinhead." (CS, Ch. 12) Crabbe and Goyle snigger when they learn that Draco's father had lied about how horribly Draco was injured by Buckbeak to ensure that the hippogriff would be punished or killed. (PA, Ch. 14) Harry and Ron snigger when Prof. Trelawney explains how Pluto could disrupt everyday life. (GF, Ch. 21) Crabbe sniggers when Harry complains about a report in *The Daily Prophet* that Crabbe supposedly got injured by a flobberworm in Hagrid's class. (GF, Ch. 24)

Snubbed - Rejected or insulted. Harry understands that he is not being snubbed when Dumbledore declines to explain his blackened hand because Dumbledore says the tale would require time to tell. (HBP, Ch. 4)

Sodden - Soaking wet. Harry's sodden robes weigh him down as he munches gillyweed and walks into the lake. (GF, Ch. 26)

Sojourn - A temporary stay. Fred and George force Montague into a vanishing cabinet, and he has a difficult sojourn in a bathroom. (OP, Ch. 30)

Solace - Relief from grief or anxiety. Slughorn says at Aragog's funeral that he hopes "your human friends find solace for the loss they have sustained." (HBP, Ch. 22)

Solemnly - Seriously. "I solemnly swear I am up to no good" are the words one speaks to get the Marauder's Map to reveal itself. (PA, Ch. 10)

Solicitously - Full of kindly concern. Dumbledore solicitously asked Harry how he felt after apparating to the Burrow. (HBP, Ch. 4)

Somber - Serious and sad. Prof. McGonagall wore such a somber expression when summoning Harry to her office that "Harry thought someone must have died." (PA, Ch. 9) Before attending Aragog's funeral, Slughorn decides his tie might be a bit too *exuberant* for the occasion and changes into a somber black *cravat*. (HBP, Ch. 22)

Soporific - Sleep-inducing. Prof. Binn's voice has soporific power. (OP, Ch. 12)

Sordid - Immoral, filthy or vile. Aunt Petunia *obsessively* follows news about a celebrity divorce even though she pretends not to be interested in such sordid affairs. (OP, Ch. 1) Prof. Trelawney views her subject as above anything so sordid as exams. (OP, Ch. 12)

Sourly - In a discontented or disagreeable way. After Ginny tells

Hermione that Harry and Ron have both been turned down by the girls they asked to the Yule Ball, Ron responds sourly. (GF, Ch. 22)

Sparse - Few in number and spread out. When he hears Lord Voldemort's voice, Frank Bryce feels the sparse hairs on the back of his neck stand up. (GF, Ch. 1)

Specimen - Example or sample. Harry recalls that when Lupin was teaching Defense Against the Dark Arts, he would often *procure* specimens of various kinds of dark creatures. (GF, Ch. 20)

Spectral - Ghostly. The Grim is a described by Prof. Trelawney as a "giant, spectral dog." (PA, Ch. 6)

Speculating - Guessing. Harry, Ron and Hermione spend a break speculating on what Dumbledore might want to teach Harry in his private lessons. (HBP, Ch. 9)

Speculation - Belief based on sketchy information. *The Daily Prophet* reports that "speculation is *rife*" that a disturbance at the Hall of Prophecy involved a prophecy about Harry Potter. (HBP, Ch. 3)

Splay - Apart. Crookshanks lands "splay-legged" after jumping after Scabbers. (PA, Ch. 4)

Sporadic - Occurring occasionally or randomly. At the Burrow, there are sporadic howls from the ghoul who lives in the attic. (GF, Ch. 10)

Splotched - Stained. Hermione learns how to make Polyjuice Potion from a splotched page of a book. (CS, Ch. 12)

Spotted dick - In England, a dessert made of pudding and dried fruit. Occasionally spotted dick is served at meals at Hogwarts. (GF, Ch. 12)

Sputtering - Babbling. After Voldemort accuses of him of wanting to abandon him, Wormtail is reduced to sputtering. (GF, Ch. 1)

Squalid - Dirty, grimy. In the Gaunt home, Harry sees a shelf of squalid-looking pots and pans. (HBP, Ch. 10)

Squat - Short and wide. Mundungus Fletcher is a squat, unshaven wizard. (OP, Ch. 2)

Squeamish - Easily grossed-out. Prof. Sprout urges her students not to be squeamish about squeezing *pulsating* green pods. (HBP, Ch. 14)

Stagnation - State of not making any progress. In her opening speech to Hogwarts students, Umbridge says change is necessary because without it there is stagnation. (OP, Ch. 11)

Stampede - Moving in a mad rush, like a herd of cattle. After a series of attacks in Book Two, there is a stampede to book seats on the Hogwarts Express. (CS, Ch. 12)

Stave off - Hold off or prevent. Harry flew close to the Horntail but not so close as to prompt her to breathe fire in order to stave him off. (GF, Ch. 20)

Steeling - Preparing for an unpleasant or difficult task. Hermione pauses, as if steeling herself, before asking everyone in the D.A. to make a commitment to the group by signing a piece of parchment. (OP, Ch. 16)

Steely - Tough, resembling steel. Describing her plan for using Polyjuice Potion, Hermione had a steely *glint* in her eye that reminded Harry of Prof. McGonagall. (CS, Ch. 12)

Sternly - In a serious, steady way. Hermione sternly tells Harry he ought to write to Sirius about the odd way he found himself in the Triwizard Tournament. (GF, Ch. 18)

Stifle - Make quiet. Harry stifles a yawn with the back of his hand, but Molly Weasley saw it and insisted he go to bed. (HBP, Ch. 5)

Stifling - Hot and stuffy, making it hard to breathe. Prof. Trelawney's classroom is stifling because it has a fire in the fireplace that Harry senses is *emitting* both heat and a "heavy, sickly sort of perfume." (PA, Ch. 8)

Stigma - A mark of bad reputation. Percy urges Ron to *sever* ties with Harry because, he says, there is a stigma that comes with associating allies of Dumbledore. (OP, Ch. 14)

Stile - A set of steps for passing over a wall or fence. Sirius tells Harry to meeting him at the stile at the end of the road out of Hogsmeade and to bring as much food as he is able. (GF, Ch. 27)

Stimulant - Something that wakes you up. Seeing the dark mark seems to act like a stimulant on Dumbledore, who bends low over his broom and speeds toward Hogwarts. (HBP, Ch. 26)

Stoically - Without complaint about pain or discomfort. Dean Thomas stoically takes the news that he is being benched in Quidditch, but Harry worries that he and Seamus are muttering *mutinously* behind his back. (HBP, Ch. 24)

Stooge - Someone who serves as a puppet to powerful person. Snape says Voldemort did not seek his help in obtaining the Sorcerer's Stone because, like everyone else, he assumed Snape was Dumbledore's stooge. (HBP, Ch. 2)

Stoutly - Firmly. When asked by Rita Skeeter if Care of Magical Creatures is one of his favorite subjects, Harry stoutly says "yes." (GF, Ch. 24)

Stragglers - Last to come or last to leave. In preparation for his conference with Sirius in the Gryffindor common room, Hermione and Harry come up with ideas on how to get stragglers out of the common room. (GF, Ch. 19)

Strategic - Having to do with a well-thought out plan. By checking the Marauder's Map at strategic *intervals*, Harry could be sure that no one was approaching the prefect's bathroom while he tested Cedric's suggestion about solving the riddle of the egg. (GF, Ch. 25)

Strategy - Idea on how to accomplish something. Harry tries to anger Ron as a way of *provoking* him to adopt a *defiant*, goal-saving attitude, but this strategy doesn't work. (HBP, Ch. 14)

Stricken - Strongly affected or overcome. Hermione looks stricken when she thinks Harry wants to go after Sirius Black in an act of revenge. (PA, Ch. 11)

Strife - Conflict. The Sorting Hat sings in Harry's fifth year at Hogwarts that there was little strife among Hogwarts' founders at first, but then *discord* crept in. (OP, Ch. 11)

Stringent - Strict. To become an Auror, one must pass stringent tests of character and magical skill. (OP, Ch. 29) Ministry of Magic officials refused to tell *The Daily Prophet* about its stringent new security plans amid rumors that Voldemort had returned. (HBP, Ch. 3)

Strut - Walk proudly, with an air of being better than other people. Harry rejects Snape's description of his father strutting around Hogwarts, saying, "My father didn't strut!" (PA, Ch. 14)

Stupendous - Incredible. With a stupendous effort, Sirius Black is able to shut curtains over the screaming portrait of his mother. (OP, Ch. 4)

Stupor - The state of being stunned or empty of energy. Harry sank in to stupor as Oliver Wood *droned* on about Quidditch *tactics*. (CS, Ch. 7)

Stymied - Prevented from achieving something. Harry desire to build a theory to explain Malfoy's strange behavior is stymied when Hermione notes that Filch's secrecy sensors would have prevented Draco from bringing any dark objects to Hogwarts. (HBP, Ch. 11)

Subconsciously - Doing something without being aware of it. Harry subconsciously finds himself planning lessons even though he had not yet agreed to teach his own version of a Defense Against the Dark Arts class. (OP, Ch. 16)

Subdue - Defeat or quiet down. Dragon keepers rush in to subdue the Horntail. (GF, Ch. 20)

Subdued - More quiet than usual. Ron is subdued after Snape insults him for his inability to apparate. (HBP, Ch. 21)

Subsided - Stopped. Harry notices that Kreacher's bitter mutterings had subsided, and that he was taking orders more *docilely*. (OP, Ch. 24)

Substandard - Poor. Prof. Trelawney reveals that Dolores Umbridge has rated her as substandard in teaching. (OP, Ch. 17)

Subtlety (pronounced "suttle-tee") - Ability to sense fine *distinctions* or do things in an understated way. Snape says Harry lacks subtlety when he describes legilimancy as mind-reading. (OP, Ch. 24)

Subversive - Working against the established order. After Griselda Marchbanks resigns in protest of the appointment of a Hogwarts High Inquisitor, *The Daily Prophet* prints an article detailing Marchbanks' "links to subversive goblin groups." (OP, Ch. 15)

Succession - Series of things or people that come one after another. Rita Skeeter writes that Hagrid has been subjecting his students to a succession of *horrific* creatures in his class at Hogwarts. (GF, Ch. 24)

Successor - A person who takes over an office or role, replacing another person. After being *sacked*, Cornelius Fudge introduces the Prime Minister to his successor, Rufus Scrimgeour. (HBP, Ch. 1)

Succinctly - In a few, well-chosen words. "Told you," Hermione says succinctly after Romilda Vane asks Harry to try a gillywater. (HBP, Ch. 15)

Succulent - Delicious. Honeydukes sells succulent-looking sweets. (PA, Ch. 10) Slughorn looks at Harry as if he is a succulent piece of pheasant. (HBP, Ch. 7)

Succumbed - Gave in to or was defeated by. Voldemort finds it hard to believe his mother could have been a witch if she had succumbed to death. (HBP, Ch. 17)

Suffused - Spread. A flush suffused Snape's face when Sirius politely informed him that he should not give Harry orders within the walls of 12 Grimmauld Place. (OP, Ch. 24)

Sulkily - In a way that suggests a person is quietly nursing hurt feelings. When Harry, Ron and Hermione encounter Moaning Myrtle at Sir Nicholas' "deathday" party, she returns their greeting sulkily. (CS, Ch. 8)

Sulky - Unhappy, feeling sorry for oneself. Parvarti Patil appeared to be enjoying herself at the Yule Ball, but Padma looked sulky. (GF, Ch. 23)

Sullen - In a bad mood. When Snape takes over Lupin's class, everyone complies with his order to turn to page 394, but with some sullen muttering. (PA, Ch. 9)

Sultry - Hot and humid. At the end of May, the weather at Hogwarts became sultry. (PA, Ch. 16)

Summons - A demand that someone show up at a certain place and time. Kreacher does not respond to Sirius' summons. (OP, Ch. 22)

Sumptuous - Delicious. Chocolate pudding at the Weasleys is described as sumptuous. (PA, Ch. 4)

Supercilious - Suspicious, doubting. When Harry explains that he created a Patronus in order to fight dementors in Little Whinging, Fudge looks supercilious and calls Harry's explanation "a very well-rehearsed story." (OP, Ch. 8) Zacharias Smith is supercilious when he hears Harry claim that he is taking Remedial Potions with Snape. (OP, Ch. 24)

Suppressed - Held back a sound or action. Harry suppressed a laugh as he gazed at all the sweets in Honeydukes. (PA, Ch. 10) Weeds grow in the Riddle family garden despite Frank Bryce's attempts to suppress them. (GF, Ch. 1) The Prime Minister is unable to suppress a plea that Fudge and Scrimgeour simply use magic to defeat Voldemort. (HBP, Ch. 1) Harry cannot suppress a suspicion that Dumbledore rather enjoys the discomfort that the Dursleys display in the company of the powerful wizard. (HBP, Ch. 3) Hermione responds to Ron's concern that Rita Skeeter has portrayed her unfavorably by emitting a suppressed laugh. (GF, Ch. 27)

Surly - Crabby. Surly security trolls pace the corridor in a *menacing* group, talking in grunts and "comparing the size of their clubs." (PA, Ch. 14) Ron spends a lot of time being surly with Hermione. (HBP, Ch. 14)

Surpassing - Going beyond. Ron's *malfunctioning* wand was surpassing itself by shooting out of Ron's grasp and hitting Prof. Flitwick. (CS, Ch. 7)

Surreptitiously - Secretly, sneakily. Embarrassed that his wand has finger marks while Cedric's is freshly polished, Harry surreptitiously tries to clean it with his robe. (GF, Ch. 18) The Prime Minister surreptitiously and superstitiously touches wood as he wishes that there will never be a murder on the premises of his government offices. (HBP, Ch. 1) Fred brags about his Decoy Detonators, which one can drop surreptitiously to create a *diversion*. (HBP, Ch. 6) Harry surreptitiously folds down the page of Advanced Potion Making on which the Half-Blood Prince had scribbled a curse because he did not want Hermione to realize what he was doing. (HBP, Ch. 21)

Suspended - Forced to leave temporarily. After Lucius Malfoy threatens to curse members of the Hogwarts Board of Directors, they vote to suspend Dumbledore. (CS, Ch. 18)

Sustained - Kept going. The *prospect* of speaking face-to-face with Sirius is all that sustained Harry before the first task in the Triwizard Tournament. (GF, Ch. 19)

Swarthy - Dark-colored. In Gringotts Bank, Harry notices that the first goblin he sees has a "swarthy, clever face." (SS, Ch. 5)

Swathed - Wearing. Lucius Malfoy strides into Hagrid's hut swathed in a black traveling cloak. (CS, Ch. 15)

Swilled - Shook in a circular motion. Harry and Ron swilled their teacups, drained them, then tried to find patterns in the soggy bits of tea leaves in the bottom of the cup. (PA, Ch. 6)

Swotty - In England, studious or nerdy. After Dudley gets bad marks in school, Uncle Vernon brushes it off, saying, he didn't want "some swotty little *nancy* boy for a son anyway." (GF, Ch. 3)

Sycophantically - In the manner of a person who is sucking up to or trying very hard to please someone else. When Malfoy insults Harry, Crabbe and Goyle laugh sycophantically. (GF, Ch. 18)

Symptoms - Signs of sickness. Hermione gives Harry a funny look as if strange symptoms might *manifest* at any moment. (HBP, Ch. 5)

Taciturn - Quiet, reserved. As the date that Harry would return to Hogwarts approached, Sirius became *prone* to being taciturn and sad. (OP, Ch. 24)

Tactful - A kind and polite way of making a point. Harry thought Mad-Eye Moody was very tactful when he gave Neville a book on magical water plants and told him that Prof. Sprout had praised his talent in Herbology. (GF, Ch. 14)

Tactics - Specific actions needed to achieve a goal. Before a Quidditch match with Hufflepuff, Oliver Wood reviews tactics. (CS, Ch. 14)

Tactless - Insensitive. Ron is tactless when he *interrogates* Cho Chang about how long she has supported her Quidditch team. (OP, Ch. 12) Moaning Myrtle tells Harry it is tactless to talk about breathing in front of her. (GF, Ch. 25)

Tad - A bit. Gilderoy Lockhart *paternally* advises Harry that handing out signed pictures can look a tad *bigheaded*. (CS, Ch. 6)

Taking the mickey - In England, laughing at someone in such a way as to make them appear foolish. When Luna Lovegood is bowled over with laughter at something Ron said, he asks if she is making fun of him by saying, "Are you taking the mickey?" (OP, Ch. 10)

Tankard - A tall mug with a lid. Hagrid drinks from a pewter tankard. (PA, Ch. 6)

Tantalizing - Attractive but impossible to attain, creating both desire and frustration. Ron and Hermione's letters give no information to Harry but only tantalizing hints, such as, "We're quite busy, but I can't give details here." (OP, Ch. 1)

Tantamount - Almost the same as. Slughorn tells Harry he does not want to accept a teaching post at Hogwarts because this would be tantamount to declaring he is allied with the Order of the Phoenix, and then Voldemort might come after him. (HBP, Ch. 4)

Tantrums - Wild, violet outbursts. Dudley has tantrums when the Dursleys decide he needs to lose weight. (GF, Ch. 3)

Tap - A faucet attached to a barrel of water, beer or other liquid. At the Quidditch World Cup, Harry sees a *queue* of people at a tap. (GF, Ch. 7)

Taradiddles - Lies, nonsense. When Harry states that he saw dementors in Little Whinging, Fudge says he doesn't have time for such taradiddles. (OP, Ch. 8)

Tarnish - Stain. "No amount of mud, wind, or rain could tarnish Harry's wonderful vision of finally winning the huge, silver Quidditch Cup." (PA, Ch. 8)

Tarry - Delay. The mermaids and mermen sing to Harry, "Your times' half-gone, so tarry not/Lest what you seek stays here to rot." (GF, Ch. 26)

Taunted - Teased. The Kwikspell letter asks, "Ever been taunted for your *woeful* wandwork?" (CS, Ch. 8)

Technicality - Picky, unpersuasive reason. Percy thinks Harry avoided being punished for his unauthorized casting of the Patronus spell because of a technicality. (OP, Ch. 14)

Technique - Way of doing something. Ron's goal-tending technique becomes wilder in Quidditch as he grows more nervous, and eventually he punches Demelza Robins in the mouth. (HBP, Ch. 14)

Tedious - Annoyingly repetitive and boring. Snape invites Bellatrix LeStrange to explain why she distrusts him and says he thinks settling this point will end her tedious interruptions of him. (HBP, Ch. 2)

Teeming - Crowded. After class, Hogwart's corridors were teeming with students. (CS, Ch. 9)

Temptation - State of being drawn to do something or be somewhere. Horace Slughorn looks as if he is trying to avoid temptation when Dumbledore offers him a teaching position at Hogwarts. (HBP, Ch. 4)

Temptress - A woman whose good looks and confident manner draws men to her. In a poetic turn of phrase, Dumbledore compares adventure to an attractive but unpredictable woman: "Let us step out into the night and pursue that flighty *temptress*, adventure." (HBP, Ch. 3)

Tentatively - Cautiously, with a degree of uncertainty. Mr. Weasley tentatively suggests to Ludo Bagman that perhaps it is time for the ministry to investigate the disappearance of Bertha Jorkins. (GF, Ch. 7)

(On) **tenterhooks** - To be "on tenterhooks" is to be nervous. After Sir Nicholas invites Harry to his deathday party, he waits on tenterhooks for Harry's reply. (CS, Ch. 8) Harry is on tenterhooks waiting for Ron to cast a spell at him in class. (HBP, Ch. 9)

Tersely - In very few words. Oliver Wood tersely calls a team meeting before a Quidditch match with Slytherin by saying, "Locker rooms." (PA, Ch. 15)

Testily - In an unpleasant and annoyed way. Hermione speaks testily about Barty Crouch, who was so merciless with his own son. (GF, Ch. 29)

Tetchy - Cranky, easily annoyed. Hermione is tetchy after *The Daily Prophet* prints lies about her and Viktor Krum. (GF, Ch. 27)

Tethered - Tied. Harry and Hermione find Buckbeak tethered outside Hagrid's cabin. (PA, Ch. 20)

Therein - In a particular place or respect. Snape explains that Dumbledore has never stopped trusting him "and therein lies my great value to the Dark Lord." (HBP, Ch. 2)

Thick - Thick-headed; stupid. "Don't be thick," Ron says after Harry suggests that maybe Dumbledore doesn't share information with Harry because he doesn't trust him. (OP, Ch. 4)

Thicker - More thick-headed. Hermione says Pansy Parkinson is "thicker than a *concussed* troll." (OP, Ch. 10)

Threadbare - Worn and shabby. The carpets at 12 Grimmauld Place are threadbare. (OP, Ch. 23)

Threshold - The flooring contained in the front entrance of a house or place of business. When Dumbledore crosses the threshold the orphanage that houses Tom Riddle wearing a suit of plum velvet, the matron looks as if a giraffe had just walked in. (HBP, Ch. 13)

Throng - Crowd. Harry avoids conversing with Colin Creevy because they are *shunted* in opposite directions by the throng of students in the corridor. (CS, Ch. 9)

Throwaway - Unimportant. Harry sees in Snape's pensieve that after James Potter argues with Lily Evans, James asks, "What is it with her?" in a way that suggests it is not just a throwaway line. (OP, Ch. 28)

Thumbscrews - Torture devices. Harry imagines that Filch would favor use of thumbscrews to promote timely arrival of students. (HBP, Ch. 8)

Thunderstruck - Struck silent by an astonishing piece of news. As Harry enters the Great Hall with his Firebolt, he is pleased to notice that everyone looks thunderstruck. (PA, Ch. 13)

Thwarted - Stopped, held back. Harry wonders what weapon Voldemort sought and whether the Order had thwarted him in his attempts to obtain it. (OP, Ch. 18) Snape admits to Bellatrix LeStrange that when Quirrell was seeking the Sorcerer's Stone, he did all he could to thwart him because at the time he had no idea that Voldemort was sharing Quirrell's body. (HBP, Ch. 2)

Tic - A small, unintended movement of a muscle that is repeated, such as a blink. When Filch is really mad, there is a tic in his cheek. (CS, Ch. 8)

Tinge - Color. Malfoy has a grayish tinge to his skin. (HBP, Ch. 15)

Tirade - A long, angry speech. After they leave a class taught by Snape, Harry launches into a tirade about Snape's behavior. (PA, Ch. 9)

Titchy - In England, a child's word for tiny. Ron calls first year students titchy. (OP, Ch. 11)

Titter - Laugh in a stressed-out or suppressed way. Prof. Trelawney emits a drunken titter when Firenze's name is mentioned. (HBP, Ch. 15)

Toddle - Take a stroll. After Prof. Lockhart removes bones from Harry's arms instead of repairing them, he suggests Harry toddle up to the hospital wing. (CS, Ch. 10)

Tolerate - Put up with. Uncle Vernon screams at Harry that he will not tolerate owls flying into his house. (OP, Ch. 2) Dumbledore informs a young Tom Riddle that thieving is not tolerated at Hogwarts. (HBP, Ch. 13)

Tormented - Hurt or made miserable. Longtime Riddle family employee Frank Bryce believed that townspeople tormented him because they believed him to be a murderer. (GF, Ch. 1)

Torpor - Sluggishness, inactivity, boredom. After Prof. Binns finished talking about the Chamber of Secrets, the History of Magic class fell back into its usual torpor. (CS, Ch. 9)

Tragic - Terrible. Rita Skeeter describes Harry as *"deprived* of love since the tragic *demise* of his parents." (GF, Ch. 27)

Trainer - In England, sneaker. Harry thinks Malfoy caught a glimpse of his trainer while he was hiding under his invisibility cloak in the Slytherin's carriage on the Hogwarts Express. (HBP, Ch. 7)

Traipsing - Walking. During the Easter holiday of Harry's fifth year, the weather is bad and Harry finds himself going nowhere other than traipsing back and forth to the library. (OP, Ch. 29)

Traitorous - Disloyal. Voldemort replaces Wormtail's hand even though he calls Wormtial worthless and traitorous. (GF, Ch. 33)

Translucent - Semi-clear, allowing light to shine through. At the deathday party, Harry sees lots of translucent figures floating about. (CS, Ch. 8)

Transpired - Occurred or became known to occur. Kreacher, it transpired, had been in the attic of 12 Grimmauld Place. (OP, Ch. 24)

Travesty - Bad imitation. Nagini was curled up before the fire like a travesty of a pet dog. (GF, Ch. 1) Dumbedore says he coerced Slughorn into giving him a memory, but its only a travesty of a recollection. (HBP, Ch. 17)

Treacherous - Disloyal. Harry is puzzled by Moody's curiosity about whether Voldemort forgave the "treacherous cowards" among the Death Eaters who never looked for Voldemort.. (GF, Ch. 35)

Treachery - Secret actions in which one does something that hurts one's leader or organization. Filch wants to show the Triwizard egg that he found to Dumbledore as evidence of the treachery of Peeves, whom he suspects stole the egg from a Triwizard champion. (GF, Ch. 25) Snape says people have gossiped falsely about his supposed treachery to the Dark Lord. (HBP, Ch. 2) After Viktor Krum says he was attacked by Barty Crouch, Karkaroff bellows, "Treachery!" (GF, Ch. 28)

Treacle - In England, molasses. Hagrid sends Harry some treacle fudge for Christmas (CS, Ch. 12) Mr. Weasley puts treacle on his porridge. (GF, Ch. 6)

Trembling - Shaking. With her hand trembling, Hermione places some of Millicent Bulstrode's hair in her Polyjuice Potion. (CS, Ch. 12)

Tremulously - With a shaky voice or movement, indicating nervousness. When Prof. Trelawney asks Neville if his grandmother is well, he answers her tremulously. (PA, Ch. 6) Aunt Petunia's voice is tremulous when she serves Dudley grapefruit as part of a new diet. (GF, Ch. 3) Winky's gaze is tremulous when Mr. Diggory questions her about the Dark Mark. (GF, Ch. 9) Hermione tremulously tells Hagrid that she and her friends missed him when he appears after a long absence (HBP, Ch. 11).

Trepidation - Fear. With some trepidation, Harry opened a present that Mrs. Weasley had bought for him. (GF, Ch. 10)

Trespass - Entering someone else's property. Sir Cadogan accuses Harry, Ron and Hermione and Ron of trespass when he notice him in a painting and he is embarrassed about having fallen off his horse. (PA, Ch. 6) Death Eaters who create a disturbance in the Hall of Prophecy are later convicted of trespass and stealing. (HBP, Ch. 3)

Trifle - A dessert, often involving sponge cake, custard, or jelly and whipped cream. Hagrid is so pleased with Harry and Ron for their roles in defeating Voldemort and rescuing Ginny at the end of Book II that he *cuffs* them on the shoulders, and they fall into their plates of trifle. (CS, Ch. 18)

Trifles - Small, unimportant matters. "Quidditch matches weren't called off for trifles like thunderstorms." (PA, Ch. 9)

Tripe - Nonsense, or a dish made from the stomach of a cow. After persuading Prof. Trelawney to become the 13th guest at a table, Prof. McGonagall offers her tripe from a *tureen*. (PA, Ch. 11) Snape complains that he doesn't want any tripe in the essays he's assigned. (HBP, Ch. 21)

Triumphant - Celebrating victory. In a triumphant voice, Ron jumps to the conclusion that Lucius Malfoy opened the Chamber of Secrets. (CS, Ch. 11)

Trivial - Unimportant. Firenze says human predictions based on the stars tend to be focused on the trivial. (OP, Ch. 27)

Tropical - From the warm-weather area between the Tropic of Cancer and the Tropic of Capricorn. Hedwig regarded tropical birds sent by Sirius as *intruders*. (GF, Ch. 2)

Troupe - Group of entertainers. On Halloween, there were rumors that a troupe of dancing skeletons would perform. (CS, Ch. 8)

Tumblers - Drinking glasses. Harry, Ron and Hermione drink Polyjuice Potion from tumblers. (CS, Ch. 12)

Tumultuous - Roaring, in a quick outburst. When Gryffindor and Hufflepuff Quidditch teams take the field, they are greeted with tumultuous applause. (CS, Ch. 14) The same occurs at the start of Gryffindor's match with Ravenclaw. (PA, Ch. 13)

Tureen - A serving bowl. After persuading Prof. Trelawney to become the 13th guest at a table, Prof. McGonagall offers her *tripe* from a tureen. (PA, Ch. 11)

Turncoat - A person who switches sides. Hagrid calls Sirius Black a turncoat. (PA, Ch. 10)

Turquoise - Blue-green. Madame Rosmerta wears turquoise high heel shoes. (PA, Ch. 10)

Tussle - Fight. *The Daily Prophet* reports that Mr. Weasley got in a tussle with Muggle policemen.

Twitchy - On edge. Hermione calls Draco Malfoy a "twitchy little ferret" after he nervously checks to see whether Prof. Moody is behind him. (GF, Ch. 23)

Unabashed - Not embarrassed. Horace Slughorn is remarkably unabashed for a man who had just been discovered pretending to be an armchair. (HBP, Ch. 4)

Unaccountably - Without explanation. Harry feels unaccountably nervous when meeting with Dumbledore. (CS, Ch. 18)

Unassailable - Unable to be disputed. With the triumphant air of a man reaching an unassailable conclusion, Uncle Vernon assumes that Harry was attacked by dementors because he had committed a crime and belongs in wizard prison. (OP, Ch. 2)

Unbalanced - Insane or overly emotional, and hence unreliable. After Cornelius Fudge reports that Voldemort has returned, *The Daily Prophet* says Harry Potter, previously viewed as unbalanced, had honorably stuck to his story. (OP, Ch. 37)

Unbiased - Even-handed. Prof. McGonagall warns Lee Jordan that he must commentate on Quidditch matches in an unbiased way. (PA, Ch. 15)

Unbidden - Without invitation. The image of the huge dog reappears in Harry's mind unbidden. (PA, Ch. 4)

Unblemished - Perfect, unmarked. After Moody performs the Adava Kedavra curse on a spider, Harry sees that its body is unmarked and wonders if his parent's bodies were unblemished after Voldemort cursed them. (GF, Ch. 14)

Uncanny - Incredibly good or accurate. Fred does an uncanny impersonation of Percy. (PA, Ch. 10) Snape says the *resemblance* between Harry and his father is uncanny, because they are both *arrogant*. (PA, Ch. 14) Dumbledore says Slughorn has an uncanny knack for picking favorite students who go on to high achievements in various fields. (HBP, Ch. 4) Slughorn compliments Tom Riddle on his uncanny ability to know things that he shouldn't and his careful *flattery* of people who count. (HBP, Ch. 23)

Unceremoniously - Simply and without fuss. When Prof. Trelawney cannot gain access to the Room of Requirement to hide her liquor bottles, she unceremoniously dumps them in a vase. (HBP, Ch. 25)

Unchallenged - Undisputed. Harry pretends he is in a bad mood because of exams, and this goes unchallenged. (OP, Ch. 29)

Uncharacteristically - Different that usual. Hagrid is uncharacteristically serious when he talks to Harry about how he and Ron have been ignoring Hermione. (PA, Ch. 14)

Unchecked - Free, unrestrained. Ivy grows unchecked over the Riddle house. (GF, Ch. 1) Rita Skeeter writes in *The Daily Prophet* that there was *lax* security" at the Quidditch World Cup and that dark wizards ran unchecked. (GF, Ch. 10)

Unctuous - An unflattering description of a person who is oily, slippery or smooth. Igor Karkaroff has a fruity, unctuous voice. (GF, Ch. 15)

Undeceived - Not fooled. Molly Weasley is undeceived when Harry tries to cover up a yawn and orders him to bed. (HBP, Ch. 5)

Underestimate - Assume something is less significant than it is. Dumbledore says Rufus Scrimgeour, who has a lot of experience fighting dark wizards, won't underestimate Lord Voldemort. (HBP, Ch. 4)

Undergrowth - Small shrubs growing on a forest floor. When leading Umbridge to Grawp, Hermione tromps loudly through the undergrowth and tells Harry that making noise is part of her plan. (OP, Ch. 33)

Undermined - Worked against. Harry's idea that Ron is vital to the Quidditch team was undermined by his observation of the rest of the team huddles away from him, complaining. (HBP, Ch. 14)

Underrepresented - Used to describe a group that has little voice in decisions despite having large numbers. Hermione says house elves are shockingly underrepresented in wizard government. (GF, Ch. 14)

Undertone - In a soft voice, so as not to be overheard. Harry explains Muggle money to Mr. Weasley in an undertone, but still arouses the curiosity of Mr. Roberts, a Muggle who is renting tents at the site of the Quidditch World Cup. (GF, Ch. 7) Mr. Weasley asks Bill in an undertone to hand him *The Daily Prophet*. (GF, Ch. 10) When Hagrid says Aragog has been a bit *restive* lately, Ron says in an undertone, "Yeah, I think we saw a bit of that side of him." (HBP, Ch. 11)

Undiluted - In pure form, not watered down. Undiluted bubotuber pus is dangerous to bare skin, Prof. Sprout says. (GF, Ch. 13)

Unearthed - Discovered. Rita Skeeter says *The Daily Prophet* has unearthed evidence that Hagrid is not a pure-blood wizard. (GF, Ch. 24)

Unease - Discomfort. Harry notices Stan looking at his forehead with unease. (PA, Ch. 3)

Unfathomable - Impossible to be read or understood. Snape's expression is unfathomable as Umbridge begins interviewing him about his experience teaching at Hogwarts. (OP, Ch. 17)

Unfazed - Unaffected. Luna Lovegood is unfazed by her Gryffindor friends' insistence that Hagrid is a good teacher; her steadiness in her opinion shows her tendency to speak uncomfortable truths. (OP, Ch. 11) The Prime Minister puts on an unfazed expression before Cornelius Fudge arrives. (HBP, Ch. 1)

Unflatteringly - In a way that makes someone look bad. Madam Pince carries a lamp that illuminates her hooked nose in a most unflattering way. (HBP, Ch. 15)

Unflinching - Unwavering, steadfast. Prof. Trelawney applauds her students for their unflinching acceptance of the horrors contained in their predictions about their future. (GF, Ch. 15) Harry meets Snape's eyes unflinchingly and tries to allow him to read his mind. (OP, Ch. 32)

Unfounded - Without any supporting evidence. When Mrs. Weasley wonders if Fred and George are planning to restart Weasley's Wizard Wheezes, Fred protests this question as an unfounded accusation. (GF, Ch. 10) Prof. Trelawney says Dolores Umbridge's inspection report is full of unfounded accusations. (OP, Ch. 17)

Unfurled - Unrolled a rolled-up piece of paper or fabric. While preparing to leave the Dursleys, Harry unfurled a message from Mr. Weasley insisting he stay put. (OP, Ch. 2)

Ungainly - Awkward. Harry slipped on the staircase, made an ungainly wobble and dropped his egg, which fell with loud noises down the steps and then burst open. (GF, Ch. 25)

Ungraciously - Lacking courtesy. Horace Slughorn agrees ungraciously to allow Dumbledore to stay for a drink at the Muggle house in which Slughorn had been living. (HBP, Ch. 4)

Unhinged - Driven mad. Harry assumes being in Azkaban unhinged Sirius Black, but he cannot understand why Prof. Lupin appears to agree with his wild tale about Peter Pettigrew. (PA, Ch. 18) Harry wonders how many people are going to suggest that he has become unhinged. (OP, Ch. 11)

Unimpeded - Unblocked. When Harry and Hermione had an unimpeded view of the street from Fred and George's shop, they noticed Draco Malfoy going somewhere alone. (HBP, Ch. 6)

Unintelligible - Unable to be understood. At one time Cornelius Fudge's comment about the dementors would have been unintelligible to the Prime Minister, but after several visits the Muggle minister understood the remark and knew it was bad news. (HBP, Ch. 1)

Unintentional - Accidental, not intended. Dumbledore says Draco Malfoy's unintentional victims were not killed, making it possible for Draco to be accepted back into law-abiding wizardry. (HBP, Ch. 27)

Unison - Together, as one. "Shut up," Uncle Vernon and Aunt Petunia roar in unison. (OP, Ch. 2)

Unnerved - Uncertain, hesitant, afraid. Tom Riddle looks unnerved when Dumbledore orders him to fetch a box containing objects he knows to be stolen. (HBP, Ch. 13)

Unobtrusive - Not easily seen or detected. The tricky part about boarding a train at platform nine and three-quarters is to do so in an unobtrusive way, so that Muggles don't notice that you disappeared into a wall. (GF, Ch. 10)

Unperturbed - Not bothered, unconcerned. Harry sees a group of goblins *cackling* over a sack of gold at the Quidditch World Cup and notices they seem quite unperturbed by nearby noise and flashes of light. (GF, Ch. 9)

Unprecedented - Unusual, occurring for the first time. The Ministry of Magic passes legislation to create the post of Hogwarts High Inquisitor, giving the ministry unprecedented power to oversee Hogwarts. (OP, Ch. 15)

Unrequited - Unreturned; usually refers to affection. Dumbledore says Merope's experience with unrequited love and the *attendant* despair may have sapped her powers. (HBP, Ch. 13)

Unseasonable - Not normal for the season. There is an unseasonable chill outside when the "Minister of Muggles" has a visit from Cornelius Fudge. (HBP, Ch. 1)

Unsettled - Disturbed, uneasy. Slughorn looks unsettled when he confessed to Harry that his habit of moving from house to house had isolated him from all his friends in the wizarding world. (HBP, Ch. 4)

Unsurpassable - The best. The Firebolt is described as having "unsurpassable balance." (PA, Ch. 4)

Unswerving - Steady. Percy says officials such as Barty Crouch deserve unswerving loyalty. (OP, Ch. 10)

Untarnished - Pure, without flaw or blemish. Dumbledore says the power of an untarnished soul like Harry's is *incomparable*. (HBP, Ch. 23)

Unwelcome - Unwanted. Oliver Wood delivers the unwelcome news that Gryffindor will be playing Hufflepuff, not Slytherin, because Draco Malfoy claims his arm is too badly injured for him to play. (PA, Ch. 9)

Upholding - Maintaining, honoring. Neville says his grandmother is always concerned about upholding the family name. (GF, Ch. 12)

Uproar - State of being highly disturbed or excited. Cornelius Fudge reports the dementors are in an uproar after Sirius Black's escape. (HBP, Ch. 1)

Upturned - Directed upward. Snapes looks over his students' upturned faces. (HBP, Ch. 9)

Ushered - Brought to a destination by a guide or escort. As members of the Order of the Phoenix introduced themselves to Harry, he felt as if he had been ushered onstage. (OP, Ch. 3)

Usurping - Taking a position of authority that has not been rightfully earned. Prof. Trelawney asks Dumbledore to *banish* "the usurping nag" — Firenze. (HBP, Ch. 20)

Utmost - The upper limit; to do one's utmost is to do one's best. Harry does his utmost to keep his voice even when it becomes clear that his bodyguards from the Order of the Phoenix had let him down. (OP, Ch. 4) Snape says he has done his utmost to get Harry expelled from Hogwarts because, in Snape's opinion, Harry is a mediocre wizard who scarcely belongs at Hogwarts. (HBP, Ch. 2)

Uttered - Spoke. After she realized that she made the 13th guest for a Christmas dinner, Sibyll Trelawney uttered a kind of soft scream. (PA, Ch. 11)

Utterly - Completely. Hermione is utterly unsurprised when Harry tells her that he has learned that there are other wizarding schools besides Hogwarts. (GF, Ch. 7)

Vaguely - Slightly, unclearly. Harry notices Kreacher staring at him *avidly*, making Harry vaguely suspicious. (OP, Ch. 24)

Vain - Thinking a lot of oneself. Harry's first impression of Slughorn is that he is vain. (HBP, Ch. 4)

Valiant - Brave, heroic, with great effort. Dobby calls Harry, "So noble! So *valiant*!" (CS, Ch. 10) Harry made a valiant effort not to sound *argumentative* when discussing his destiny with Dumbledore. (HBP, Ch. 23)

Vapid - Lacking interest. In a statue inside the Ministry of Magic, Harry notices an image of witch with a vapid smile, like a beauty contestant. (OP, Ch. 9)

Vehemently - With great force and emphasis. Harry denies he placed his name in the Goblet of Fire vehemently. (GF, Ch. 17) Draco vehemently tells Dumbledore his heart has been in his service to the Dark Lord. (HBP, Ch. 27)

Venerable - Honorable. Harry sees "venerable-looking" wizards in the Leaky Cauldron. (PA, Ch. 4)

Vengeance - Getting even. Narcissa fears that Voldemort gave Draco a dangerous job as vengeance against Lucius Malfoy for his errors. (HBP, Ch. 2)

Venomous - Full of hate or evil intent. Looking at the Dark Mark, Harry felt fear grow inside him like venomous bubble. (HBP, Ch. 26)

Verge - Brink or edge. When explaining his strange dreams, Harry is on the verge of saying how felt inside Voldemort's mind, as if he were thinking Voldemort's thoughts. (GF, Ch. 10)

Veritable - Real, not imaginary. Bertha Jorkins proved to be veritable mine of information, Voldemort says. (GF, Ch. 33)

Vermin - Disgusting pests such as rats, lice or fleas. Dobby says that when Voldemort was in power, house elves were treated like vermin. (CS, Ch. 10) Sirius Black calls Peter Pettigrew a piece of vermin and tells Harry that Pettigrew is responsible for his parents' deaths. (PA, Ch. 19) Snape tells Narcissa and Bellatrix they are alone if one does not count vermin — namely, Peter Pettigrew. (HBP, Ch. 2)

Version - One of many retellings of a story. There were many versions of what happened at the Riddle house, but all the stories began with a maid entering a room and finding three members of the family dead. (GF, Ch. 1)

Vestiges - Remains. After everyone started doing magic the night before the Quidditch World Cup, ministry officials gave up any vestiges of pretending to control the situation. (GF, Ch. 7) Looking at a portrait of Bellatrix LeStrange, Harry sees vestiges of beauty. (OP, Ch. 25)

Vicinity - Area. Luna Lovegood has a hat shaped like a lion and when it roars, it makes everyone in the vicinity jump. (OP, Ch. 19) When Rufus Scrimgeour and Percy drop in on the Weasley' Christmas dinner, Scrimgeour claims they were in the vicinity on business. (HBP, Ch. 16)

Vicious - Brutal and aggressive. Ron tells Harry that it is giants' nature to be vicious. (GF, Ch. 23) Grawp is vicious. (HBP, Ch. 8)

Vigilance - Watching out for something bad that might happen. Mad-Eye Moody's motto is "Constant Vigilance." (GF, Ch. 14)

Vigorously - With energy and enthusiasm. After the Sorting Hat places Harry in Gryffindor, Percy shakes his hand vigorously. (SS, Ch. 7) Prof. Trelawney reshuffles her cards vigorously after they told her about a dark young man who disliked her; she had no idea Harry was hiding nearby. (HBP, Ch. 10)

Vindictive - Mean. After watching Harry struggle with a potion, Snape scribbled something in his notebook with "an air of vindictive pleasure." (CS, Ch. 16)

Vivacious - Lively. Slughorn tells Harry that his mother, Lily, was vivacious. (HBP, Ch. 4) Rita Skeeter describes Pansy Parkinson as a "pretty and vivacious fourth-year student." (GF, Ch. 27)

Vividly - Clearly, like a picture in one's mind. Harry can vividly remember Hagrid warning him not to stray from the path in the Forbidden Forest. (CS, Ch. 15) When Moaning Myrtle asks Harry if he remembers when she visited him in the bath, he says, "vividly." (HBP, Ch. 21)

Vociferously - Loudly and insistently. Harry overhears Beau Batons students arguing vociferously before the Dark Mark appears. (GF, Ch. 9)

Vogue - Period of popularity. Lupin recalls that the curse Levicorpus "had a great vogue during my time at Hogwarts." (HBP, Ch. 16)

Volition - Will. Harry sees two boxes moving as if of their own volition. (HBP, Ch. 20)

Voluminous - Large. Before the Dark Mark appears, Harry sees a Muggle woman floating in the air, struggling as her voluminous underwear is exposed. (GF, Ch. 9)

Vouched for - Declared to be worthy of trust. Although Karkaroff tells the Wizengamut that Snape is a Death Eater, this is ignored because Dumbledore had vouched for Snape. (GF, Ch. 30)

Vouchsafed - Entrusted with. Prof. Trelawnly babbles about "certain dark *portents* I have glimpsed" and "omens I have been vouchsafed" before Harry gets her attention by asking whether she had been trying to enter the Room of Requirement. (HBP, Ch. 25)

Waggling - Moving from side to side. At the Slytherin table, Malfoy and his friends were waggling their tongues as if they were snakes in order to taunt Harry about being a parseltongue. (GF, Ch. 31)

Wallow - To remain in a state or situation, as if you are helpless, even though you are not. In teaching Harry Occlumency, Snape warns him to wallow in emotional states such as sadness because this makes him easy prey for Voldemort's Legilimancy. (OP, Ch. 24)

Wan - Feeble. After Mr. Weasley is taken to St. Mungo's, Mrs. Weasley is able to give Harry and her sons a wan smile. (OP, Ch. 22)

Warily - With caution. At the beginning of his fourth year at Hogwarts, Harry warily greets Colin Creevey, who in the past has treated Harry like a hero. (GF, Ch. 12)

Warlock - A male wizard. In the Three Broomsticks, Madame Rosmerta serves a rowdy group of warlocks. (PA, Ch. 10)

Wary - Cautious. Harry notices that Snape seemed strangely wary of displaying *overt animosity* to Mad-Eye Moody. (GF, Ch. 14)

Waspish - Threatening and unpleasant, like a wasp. Snape walks though his class making waspish remarks about the work of Gryffindors. (CS, Ch. 11) Hermione snaps at people waspishly after *The Daily Prophet* prints lies about her and Viktor Krum. (GF, Ch. 27)

Wastrel - A person who is good for nothing. Uncle Vernon describes James Potter as a wastrel. (PA, Ch. 2)

Wavered - Fell off or hesitated. Voldemort tells Wormtail he awaits the return of his "faithful servant" whose loyalty has never wavered. (GF, Ch. 1)

Wayside - Along a path or road. Wormtail met Bertha Jorkins, a Ministry of Magic employee, at a wayside inn and brought her to Voldemort, who obtained a great deal of information from her. (GF, Ch.1)

Wending - Travel, especially down a twisty path. Hagrid stepped off the path in the Forbidden Forest and began wending his way through the trees. (OP, Ch. 30)

Wheedle - To flatter someone in an effort to get them to do something. Harry had enough experience trying to wheedle information out of people to recognize that Tom Riddle was a master at this. (HBP, Ch. 23)

Wheezy - An airy voice, almost like a whistle. Harry's mirror in his room at the Leaky Cauldron speaks to him in a wheezy voice. (PA, Ch. 4)

Whence - Where. Dumbledore describes Borgin and Burkes as the very shop from whence the necklace that injured Katie Bell came. (HBP, Ch. 13)

Whereabouts - Location of a person or object. Rita Skeeter reports that the whereabouts of Fridwulfa, Hagrid's mother, are unknown. (GF, Ch. 24)

Whim - A sudden desire. After drinking Felix Felicis, Harry got the idea that he ought to take an indirect route to Hagrids, and he follows this whim. (HBP, Ch. 22)

Winces - Facial expressions of pain. Harry ignores the winces that Ron and Hermione make every time he says, "Voldemort." (OP, Ch. 14)

Wistfully - With a sad feeling of yearning for something absent or unattainable. Bill Weasley looks wistfully at the Hogwarts Express and says he kind of wishes he were still in school. (GF, Ch. 10)

Witheringly - In a highly critical way. Rita Skeeter speaks witheringly about *The Quibbler.* (OP, Ch. 25)

Wizened - Old, shriveled. Tom, the owner of the Leaky Cauldron, is described as wizened. (PA, Ch. 3) Kreacher has a wizened arm. (HBP, Ch. 19)

Woebegone - Sad, tired, messy. Scabbers looks woebegone. (PA, Ch. 4) After a visit to Grawp, Hagrid looked woebegone. (OP, Ch. 30)

Woeful - Lousy. The Kwikspell letter asks, "Ever been *taunted* for you woeful wandwork? (CS, Ch. 8)

Woolly - Confused or lacking clearness. Hermione says she thinks Divination is "very woolly" because it involves "a lot of guesswork." (PA, Ch. 6)

Worthier - More deserving. After claiming that Harry is dating Hermione, Rita Skeeter writes that Harry's well-wishers must hope that next time he "*bestows* his heart on a worthier candidate." (GF, Ch. 27)

Wotcher - An informal term of greeting used among friends. When Tonks sees him enter The Buirrow, Tonks says, "Wotcher, Harry." (HBP, Ch. 5) Tonks also says wotcher when she rescues him from the Hogwarts Express after Malfoy's attack. (HBP, Ch. 8)

Wrath - Angry action. Voldemort warns Wormtail to be obedient or face the full *extent* of Lord Voldemort's wrath.

Wreaked - Committed an act of destruction. Nearly Headless Nick blandly reports that Peeves wreaked *havoc* and *mayhem*, as usual. (GF, Ch. 12)

Wrenched - Moved or twisted by force. Dumbledore wrenches a camera out of Colin Creevey's hands after he was petrified. (CS, Ch. 10)

Wretched - Awful. The "Minister of Muggles" is awaiting a phone call from a "wretched man" who is president of a far-off country when he hears a man in a portrait cough. (HBP, Ch. 1) Snape says he doesn't "give a damn" about Peeves, "that wretched *poltergeist.*" (GF, Ch. 25)

Writhing - Twisting in pain. The night before a Quidditch match with Slytherin, Harry's stomach was writhing. (PA, Ch. 15) Katie Bell is writhing in pain after she touched a mysterious package that she was carrying from Hogsmeade to Hogwarts. (HBP, Ch. 12)

Wrought - Brought about. A year of dieting and learning how to box had wrought a more muscular *physique* for Dudley. (OP, Ch. 1)

Wryly - Grimly humorous. Harry thought wryly that if everyone blamed him for a Quidditch loss, he had endured worse mutterings. (HBP, Ch. 14)

Yearningly— In a manner that is full of desire. Filch looks yearningly up the staircase where he think Peeves went after doing so mischief, but agrees to go with Prof. Snape instead. (GF, Ch. 25)

Yeomen - Assistants. In the portrait hole, Sir Cadogan refers to Harry and Ron as "my fine young yeomen". (PA, Ch.12)

A new edition of the Pottersaurus will be issued after publication of the seventh book in the Harry Potter series, <u>Harry Potter and the Deathly Hallows</u>. For information or to reserve your copy, visit www.pottersaurus.com.

APPENDIX
Words Organized by Book and Chapter

Harry Potter and the Sorcerer's Stone

Chapter 4
Codswallop

Chapter 5
Apothecary
Burnished
Cheek
Drawling
Infernal
Swarthy

Chapter 6
Engraved
Hurtled
Ravine

Chapter 7
Chivalry
Enviously
Oddment
Vigorously

Chapter 10
Festoons

Chapter 12
Brandishing

Chapter 13
Skulking

Chapter 17
Abysmal
Confiscated
Hygienic
Loathed
Sidled

Harry Potter and the Chamber of Secrets

Chapter 4
Abashed
Dodgy
Jaunty

Chapter 5
Cajolingly
Canopy
Indignantly
Innumerable

Chapter 6
Bigheaded

Chapter 7
Malfunctioning
Scalawag
Stupor
Surpassing

Chapter 8
Airborne
Anguished
Befouling
Bulbous
Glummest
Havoc
Hobbled
Impressive
Lank
Menace
Sulkily
Taunted
Tenterhooks
Tic
Translucent
Troupe
Woeful

Chapter 9
Abruptly
Assured
Blanched
Bracingly
Ludicrous
Maniac
Sensational
Shunted
Teeming
Throng
Torpor

Chapter 10
Clenched
Ecstasy
Escort
Meddle
Noble
Quivering
Rogue
Toddle
Valiant
Vermin
Wrenched

Chapter 11
Askew
Balaclava
Blundered
Knotgrass
Mayhem
Prodding
Pummeling
Resplendent
Triumphant
Waspish

Chapter 12
Bewildered
Bout

Breathlessly
Comeuppance
Decrepit
Derisive
Disrepute
Dollops
Doom
Frothed
Glint
Glutinous
Heir
Hitherto
Incredulously
Indistinguishable
Labyrinthine
Lacewings
Laden
Morosely
Ranting
Rasp
Skirting
Sluggishly
Smoldering
Sniggering
Splotched
Stampede
Steely
Treacle
Trembling
Tumblers

Chapter 13
Bloke
Expectant
Guffaw
Smarmiest

Chapter 14
Christened
Disembodied
Knottiest
Tactics
Tumultuous

Chapter 15
Brambles
Fretfully
Hampered
Irksome
Irresolute
Raucous
Scampering
Scuttled
Sentiments
Swathed
Vividly

Chapter 16
Blimey
Culprit
Entwined
Feeble
Pregnant
Vindictive

Chapter 17
Crimson
Daubed
Retort
Serpentine

Chapter 18
Abject
Consorted
Contrary
Cuffs
Disheveled
Impaled
Incensed
Livid
Lunged
Resentful
Serenely
Shrilly
Sleek
Suspended
Trifle
Unaccountably

*Harry Potter and
the Prisoner of
Azkaban*

Chapter 1
Emblazoned
Luminous
Medieval
Ominous
Rebound

Chapter 2
Abnormality
Apoplectic
Civil
Expulsion
Gaunt
Insolent
Layabout
Protruding
Puce
Ruddy
Scrounger
Wastrel

Chapter 3
Collywobbles
Contemptuously
Eluding
Flap
Infamous
Irritable
Massive
Unease
Wizened

Chapter 4
Aerodynamic
Cobbled
Composedly
Earnestly
Erected
Grappled
Honed

Incorporates
Loftily
Podium
Proprietor
Prototype
Replenish
Shrilly
Splay
Sumptuous
Unbidden
Unsurpassable
Venerable
Wheezy
Woebegone

Chapter 5
Befuddled
Brow
Cavernous
Dilapidated
Foreboding
Furrowed
Furtive
Infuriating
Maliciously
Perchance
Perish
Procession
Scorn

Chapter 6
Aura
Braggart
Brandishing
Crestfallen
Crinolines
Disdainful
Dreading
Dregs
Emboldened
Haughtily
Knave
Mundane
Nonchalantly

Omen
Pewter
Pouf
Receptivity
Resonances
Scabbard
Scalding
Scurvy
Spectral
Swilled
Tankard
Tremulously
Trespass
Trifles
Woolly

Chapter 8
Bloodshed
Bludgeon
Concocted
Dejectly
Dispiritedly
Flourish
Listlessly
Menacingly
Repel
Stifling
Tarnish

Chapter 9
Beckoned
Cur
Immensely
Inexplicably
Insufferable
Mangy
Pensively
Pitch
Pompous
Silhouette
Somber
Sullen
Tirade
Unwelcome

Chapter 10
Broodingly
Confiscated
Crone
Disembowelment
Evasively
Festive
Impersonation
Indignation
Levitating
Ludicrous
Manic
Marauder
Miniscule
Nicked
Opaline
Parchment
Repossessed
Solemnly
Succulent
Suppressed
Turncoat
Turquoise
Uncanny
Warlock

Chapter 11
Alight
Anonymously
Averted
Coursing
Fathom
Maddening
Orb
Packing case
Panicky
Rekindled
Relevant
Roving
Scandalized
Sequined
Stricken
Tripe
Tureen
Uttered

Chapter 12
Yeomen

Chapter 13
Indignantly
Phenomenal
Profoundly
Thunderstruck

Chapter 14
Arrogant
Brightly
Chilling
Contorted
Dank
Gloat
Malevolent
Menacing
Pirouette
Plummeted
Resemblance
Sallow
Savagely
Strut
Surly
Uncharacteristically

Chapter 15
Culminated
Dewy
Doddery
Eruption
Exuberant
Gauzy
Grim
Hoarse
Pathetic
Pursuits
Resorting
Retaliation
Rickety
Tersely
Unbiased
Writhing

Chapter 16
Appeal
Ashen-faced
Bemoaning
Clambered
Euphoria
Executioner
Flattered
Mutinous
Retrieve
Seizure
Sultry

Chapter 17
Convulsively

Chapter 18
Cringing
Unhinged

Chapter 20
Boisterous
Fervently
Huskily
Imploringly
Irresolute
Lolling
Manacle
Precautions
Tethered

Chapter 21
Jauntily

***Harry Potter and
the Goblet of Fire***

Chapter 1
Audible
Croakily
Defiantly
Derelict
Embroidering
Flickering
Flinch

Gnarled
Groped
Incoherently
Inhabitants
Invaluable
Mirthless
Obsessed
Plotting
Pottering
Pronounced
Protracted
Revolt
Sparse
Sputtering
Suppressed
Tormented
Travesty
Unchecked
Version
Wavered

Chapter 2
Disbanded
Disconcerting
Incurably
Intruders
Punctuated
Tropical

Chapter 3
Boisterous
Casually
Cogs
Curtly
Glowered
Immense
Knickerbockers
Nancy
Perusing
Refuge
Swotty
Tantrums

Chapter 4
Diatribe

Downright
Elongated
Imminent

Chapter 5
Conjure
Isolation
Sanctimoniously

Chapter 6
Diluting
Indistinctly
Manky
Roused

Chapter 7
Abided
Adorned
Bedecked
Blatant
Complied
Confection
Disentangled
Distractedly
Dubious
Embargo
Extravagant
Hillock
Hindrance
Impeccably
Inexpertly
Lumbago
Mallet
Midges
Modified
Niche
Palpable
Placidly
Preened
Proportions
Punctured
Queue
Registry
Retreated

Scrutinizing
Tap
Tentatively
Undertone
Utterly
Vestiges

Chapter 8
Awestruck
Blankly
Blighter
Cadge
Comprised
Coordinated
Descent
Feint
Forlorn
Gallant
Gesticulating
Infectious
Ploy
Resounding

Chapter 9
Amok
Buoyant
Cackling
Colossal
Disbelief
Discomforted
Emerged
Emitting
Etched
Gaggle
Grotesque
Impeded
Incantation
Misfortune
Momentarily
Parentage
Prostrating
Unperturbed
Vociferously
Voluminous

Chapter 10
Apprehended
Blunders
Cinders
Clamoring
Conspicuous
Cronies
Darning
Disorientated
Dumbstruck
Evidently
Ferreting
Formidable
Frenzy
Immersed
Lax
Moldering
Nutter
Pillock
Quibbling
Reassurance
Sporadic
Trepidation
Unfounded
Unobtrusive
Verge
Wistfully

Chapter 12
Appalled
Bedraggled
Chortled
Delegation
Embroidered
Fen
Gateau
Glen
Hoodwinks
Intensified
Moor
Presumably
Reinstate
Reminiscent
Renown
Shrewdly

Spotted dick
Upholding
Warily
Wreaked

Chapter 13
Deciphered
Deformed
Humiliation
Intermingle
Lethal
Liberal
Nonentity
Petrol
Queuing
Sarcastically
Undiluted

Chapter 14
Animosity
Assent
Distinctive
Dustbins
Forewarned
Grizzled
Inscrutably
Mane
Overt
Rampaging
Reckon
Tactful
Unblemished
Underrepresented
Vigilance
Wary

Chapter 15
Badgering
Colluding
Commending
Congregated
Gratitude
Hysterics
Oppression

Paranoid
Sacked
Unctuous
Unflinching

Chapter 16
Binding
Blancmange
Constitutes
Elephantine
Encrusted
Fawning
Gravely
Impartial
Kip
Mutilated
Prowess
Query
Rapt

Chapter 17
Cunningly
Disarray
Exempted
Imperiously
Injust
Malice
Melodramatic
Ransacked
Reverie
Skeptical
Vehemently

Chapter 18
Din
Disfigures
Ensure
Exacerbated
Gawping
Gist
Mannish
Obsolete
Patronizing
Paunchy
Precariously

Relish
Remotely
Sternly
Surreptitiously
Sycophantically

Chapter 19
Askance
Devoid
Endure
Enraptured
Fortnight
Hags
Harebrained
Haven
Perimeter
Prospect
Reverence
Stragglers

Chapter 20
Adrenaline
Barking
Clutch
Collective
Counterpart
Crescendo
Enclosure
Gouge
Imbues
Overblown
Specimen
Stave off
Subdue

Chapter 21
Addressee
Balderdash
Barmy
Confidentially
Contagious
Diversion
Flagon
Foraged
Frivolous

Peckish
Prat

Appraising
Impregnable
Sourly

Accessible
Amiably
Chamber pot
Discomposed
Dismissively
Domains
Fraternizing
Maternal
Sulky
Twitchy
Vicious

Bigotry
Bloodthirsty
Campaign
Condensation
Conscience
Controversial
Explicit
Extinction
Horrific
Hysteria
Intimidation
Moored
Notoriously
Petty
Prejudice
Quailing
Succession
Unearthed
Whereabouts

Apprehension
Distinct

Forgo
Incriminated
Intervals
Plaintively
Poltergeist
Replicas
Ungainly
Wretched

Commiserating
Lest
Tarry

Bestows
Demise
Devious
Fathomless
Fissure
Smitten
Stile
Tetchy
Tragic
Worthier

Perturbed
Pining
Quash
Scoffed

Apparition
Discarded
Excruciating
Immovable
Preamble
Premonition
Skeptical
Testily

Ascent
Heinous

Reverberate
Vouched for

Aggravating
Berserk
Converse
Naught
Waggling

Obscure
Quizzical

Traitorous
Veritable

Niceties

Cavort
Treacherous

Blustering
Envoys
Obstinate
Preceded

Formulating

*Harry Potter
and the Order
of the Phoenix*

Bespectacled
Budgie
Concealed
Consolation
Endear
Grimace

Hardened
Hooligan
Obsessively
Parched
Pestilential
Physique
Pinched
Putrid
Resultant
Scathingly
Sordid
Tantalizing
Wrought

Chapter 2
Ascertain
Breach
Burgeoned
Comprehension
Ebbing
Exasperated
Flustered
Materialized
Pending
Pretense
Rant
Squat
Tolerate
Unassailable
Unfurled
Unison

Chapter 3
Avidly
Interrogated
Interspersed
Invariably
Lethargy
Pungent
Recede
Reproachfully
Smugness
Ushered

Chapter 4
Abomination
Dulcet
Git
Insubstantial
Obscured
Peaky
Reprovingly
Stupendous
Thick
Utmost

Chapter 5
Collective
Destabilize
Discredit
Embossed
Gormless
Monotony
Prolonged
Protuberance

Chapter 6
Abated
Dolefully
Immobilized
Ingenious
Loathing
Ornate
Pacify
Permeate
Redolent

Chapter 7
Disconsolate
Extricated
Flummoxed
Regurgitate
Sepulchral

Chapter 8
Austere
Bilge
Flagrant

Fortified
Goaded
Miscarriage
Monocle
Simper
Supercilious
Taradiddles

Chapter 9
Cowering
Dismally
Dither
Ecstatic
Estrangement
Rhapsodizing
Row
Segregation
Servility
Vapid

Chapter 10
Ballistic
Bemused
Commotion
Concussed

Chapter 11
Affronted
Condemned
Dilapidated
Discord
Prominent
Selfsame
Stagnation
Strife
Titchy
Unfazed

Chapter 12
Accusatory
Asperity
Elite
Engrossed
Enmity

Mere
Mollified
Rebuffed
Secluded
Shortlisted
Skive
Soporific
Tactless

Chapter 13
Admonitory
Channeling
Misshapen
Pretext
Provocation
Reinforce
Repressively
Senile

Chapter 14
Allusions
Detritus
Flouting
Fraternization
Misguided
Obliging
Sever
Snide
Stigma
Technicality
Winces

Chapter 15
Brusquely
Churlish
Consternation
Covertly
Defiance
Delusional
Eccentric
Formalized
Mingled
Noncommittal
Objective

Prestigious
Repose
Subversive
Unprecedented

Chapter 16
Chuffed
Chunter
Foisted
Imprecations
Involuntarily
Mobilize
Steeling
Subconsciously

Chapter 17
Accusations
Addled
Congealing
Drone
Incomprehensible
Indignity
Insinuations
Klaxonlike
Monotonous
Substandard
Unfathomable

Chapter 18
Draught
Efficacious
Opaque
Respite
Ruefully
Thwarted

Chapter 19
Abstained
Accustomed
Hovel
Mimic
Morale
Obstructed
Partisan
Vicinity

Chapter 20
Ingratiating

Chapter 21
Disposed
Induce

Chapter 22
Emphatically
Gibbering
Summons
Wan

Chapter 23
Complementary
Contradicted
Deflate
Grievous
Impertinent
Mortified
Popinjay
Proffering
Regally
Threadbare

Chapter 24
Adept
Chivvying
Delegate
Distinctions
Docilely
Extract
Inadvisable
Incumbent
Incursion
Jubilant
Lamentable
Noxious
Obscure
Prone
Reformed
Subsided
Subtlety
Suffused
Taciturn

Transpired
Vaguely
Wallow

Chapter 25
Disparagingly
Witheringly

Chapter 26
Benignly
Callously
Disconsolately
Dismal
Fiasco
Languidly
Progressively

Chapter 27
Blandly
Blinkered
Contradicting
Corruption
Fettered
Impassively
Impersonal
Intimidating
Offensive
Rendered
Scrum
Trivial

Chapter 28
Account
Aspersions
Besieged
Conceited
Conspiratorially
Rebellious
Throwaway

Chapter 29
Admonitions
Berk
Demeanor

Dire
Dissuade
Intervened
Placatingly
Premises
Raving
Stringent
Traipsing
Unchallenged

Chapter 30
Animatedly
Inflection
Miscreant
Overwrought
Realization
Reverting
Saturated
Servitude
Sojourn
Wending

Chapter 31
Deferentially
Desultory
Elixir
Naive
Recurrence
Reimburse
Sedately

Chapter 32
Aghast
Contemplated
Deliberately
Despicable
Exultant
Inclination
Inflexible
Irascible
Ironic
Minions
Pinioned
Resurgence

Chapter 33
Insurmountable
Undergrowth

Chapter 36
Corpulent
Irretrievable
Precautionary

Chapter 37
Assiduously
Extensive
Grudgingly
Invincible
Slander
Unbalanced

*Harry Potter and
the Half-Blood
Prince*

Chapter 1
Aggrieved
Atrocity
Baffling
Betray
Blackmail
Boded
Careworn
Consented
Convey
Deficient
Disgorging
Encompassed
Fretful
Graver
Grueling
Hallucination
Heatedly
Ignorant
Importing
Loping
Overstatement
Predecessor
Prise

Publicity
Rangy
Rummaging
Savoring
Shrewdness
Successor
Unfazed
Unintelligible
Unseasonable
Uproar
Wretched

Chapter 2
Allegiance
Ally
Apportioning
Beseechingly
Circulating
Discomfited
Displeasure
Doused
Dunghill
Eloquent
Embraced
Encased
Fair
Fleeting
Forestalled
Gesture
Imperceptibly
Implicitly
Inclined
Indecent
Indifferently
Initial
Labyrinth
Outrage
Pitiable
Relapse
Reminiscences
Remorse
Ruthlessly
Sardonically
Stooge
Tedious

Therein
Vengeance

Chapter 3
Advised
Agitated
Appalling
Astray
Atmosphere
Bloodshot
Clarified
Colleague
Corresponded
Cowering
Encumbered
Evoked
Fabled
Flighty
Flourishing
Fraught
Fug
Inherit
Leaflet
Linger
Masquerading
Missive
Neglecting
Persistent
Possessions
Preposterous
Problematic
Rechristened
Repugnant
Residue
Retorts
Rife
Rift
Skulking
Speculation
Stringent
Temptress

Chapter 4
Absurd
Afoul of

Airily
Balefully
Coercion
Confiding
Considerable
Cosseted
Decisive
Deplore
Deprive
Derision
Dictates
Disservice
Elaborate
Encounter
Impersonated
Imposter
Intruding
Mortality rate
Notwithstanding
Pate
Proffered
Prudent
Recruiting
Redoubled
Reprimanded
Snubbed
Solicitously
Tantamount
Temptation
Unabashed
Underestimate
Ungraciously
Unsettled
Vain

Chapter 5
Awkwardly
Complacently
Contaminated
Drawn
Eloping
Emanate
Excess
Feverishly
Groggy

Manifest
Obstruction
Perpetrator
Phlegm
Procedure
Punch-drunk
Stifle
Symptoms
Undeceived
Wotcher

Chapter 6
Appreciatively
Disabuse
Dither
Flippant
Retribution
Unimpeded

Chapter 7
Anecdotes
Cloistered
Compere
Dumbfounded
Illustrious
Mesmerized
Trainer

Chapter 8
Distorted
Frenzied
Miming
Recounting
Sensitivity
Thumbscrews

Chapter 9
Aggravated
Caress
Genially
Grisly
Gruesome
Incredulity
Mutating

Portentously
Radiant
Remonstration
Speculating

Chapter 10
Besotted
Cherished
Copse
Correspondingly
Deduce
Enslaving
Indiscriminately
Knave
Lumbering
Squalid

Chapter 11
Preferential
Restive
Stymied

Chapter 12
Advisability
Bandy-legged
Dramatically
Excursion
Jibe

Chapter 13
Asylum
Attendant
Bestial
Deluded
Enigmatic
Expressionless
Feigning
Fevered
Heirloom
In due course
Inadvertently
Inquisitorial
Intrigued

Maladies
Notorious
Quaking
Threshold
Unnerved
Unrequited
Whence

Chapter 14
Blithely
Bravado
Coincided
Disoriented
Elusive
Erectly
Hypocrite
Inconsistent
Inkling
Marginally
Provoking
Pulsating
Secateurs
Squeamish
Strategy
Technique
Undermined
Wryly

Chapter 15
Agog
Befouled
Countenance
Depraved
Desecrated
Despoiled
Devoutly
Dispassionately
Embarked
Gate-crash
Incautious
Inscrutable
Juncture
Mania
Protuberant

Single-handedly
Succinctly
Tinge
Titter
Unflatteringly

Chapter 16
Deliberated
Marshal
Vogue

Chapter 17
Abstinence
Lamenting
Overindulged
Rotund
Succumbed

Chapter 18
Contemptuous
Disparate
Reverted

Chapter 19
Constricted
Exasperation
Fuming
Inaudible
Indigo
Overexert
Ruse
Sheepish

Chapter 20
Banish
Cunning
Engenders
Envisaged
Exerted
Henchmen
Inexplicable
Ingenuity
Leer
Ministrations

Oblivious
Omniscient
Outcast
Pittance
Predisposed
Pronouncements
Usurping
Volition

Chapter 21
Augury
Befits
Belligerent
Berth
Imprint
Quelled
Reanimated
Rematerialize
Shufti
Subdued

Chapter 22
Arachnid
Consolingly
Convert
Cravat
Elation
Exhilarating
Fermenting
Fractionally
Infinite
Passable
Revere
Skein
Solace
Whim

Chapter 23
Argumentative
Artifact
Caliber
Detrimental
Diminished
Explicable

Flattery
Hypothetical
Immortality
Incomparable

Incriminating
Intolerable
Magnitude
Maimed
Mortal
Untarnished
Wheedle

Chapter 24
Congealed
Harping
Inextricably
Stoically

Chapter 25
Calamity
Compressed
Ejecting
Endurance
Haughty
Impenetrable
Jocularly
Macho
Portent
Robustly
Unceremoniously
Vouchsafed

Chapter 26
Benumbed
Crude
Ineptitude
Inexorably
Peaceable
Stimulant
Venomous

Chapter 27
Accomplice

Compelled
Contamination
Conversationally
Copiously
Unintentional

Chapter 30
Otherworldly